The content of the work has been developed exclusively by members of the **Time of Software** team.

TIME
OF
SOFTWARE

November 2020

For more information, please visit:
www.timeofsoftware.com
www.aprendeenunfindesemana.com

# TABLE OF CONTENT

3

## INTRODUCTION

Welcome to the beautiful world of software programming!

You have come this far, that is because you want to learn to program correctly and do it with Python! And the best of all, you have decided to do it with us. Thank you very much!

The objective of the book is to build a solid base of programming with the Python programming language so that you can cope with any situation. To do this, we have designed a learning method based entirely on progressive practices with basic theoretical notions. We have structured it in a way that allows you to learn it in a weekend.

Suppose you finish the book and follow our learning model. In that case, you can have enough autonomy to carry out your programming projects. Or at least launch yourself to try it.

We are sure that, if you accompany us to the end of the book, you come up with a large number of ideas for programming projects. We know that since the more knowledge you learn, the more curiosity you develop and the more ideas emerge.

We encourage you to start delving into this world and enjoy each project. Do not despair if you do not get it the first time, since indeed from each mistake, you learn something that helps you keep moving forward. This book is just the beginning.

Let's start!

## WHAT DO I NEED TO GET STARTED?

To learn Python in a weekend, as we propose in the book, you need the following:

- **A computer**: if you do not have an internet connection, you have to download the Python development platform using any computer connected to the internet. After having it downloaded you have to install it on the computer that you are going to use throughout the training. In the following sections, we explain the steps to follow to install the development environment on each of the operating systems supported by the Python development platform.

And of course, just a weekend!

At the end of the book, you find the URL from where you can download the source code of all the exercises in the book.

The book is written to help you to learn Python quickly, efficiently, and with a practical approach. If you are new in programming, in the book, we are going to explain simply all the concepts you need to know to learn to program using Python. If you already know how to program, in the book, you find everything you need to know to have a solid base of the language that allows you to go deeper.

Topics covered by the book are carefully selected and arranged in a way that facilitates progressive learning of all the concepts.

The book has a straightforward, practical approach, with a multitude of examples that allow you to consolidate all the theoretical knowledge that we explain to you.

Let's see how we have organized the book.

## ORGANIZATION

There are two differentiated parts:

- **A theoretical block**: about the language and the installation of the development platform.
- **A practice block**: programming theory and practice.

The first part of the learning includes a theoretical explanation about the Python programming language. Also, everything necessary for you to be able to assemble all the software infrastructure you need to start programming with Python and the explanation of how to program with the developing environment.

The practical learning has nine different **Goals** and five **Projects**, which serve to consolidate the knowledge acquired in the other Goals.

**Goals** have incremental difficulty. When you progress with the book, you learn new knowledge of greater complexity than previous ones. Goals contain different grouped exercises that we call Phases. At the beginning of each Goal, we explain all theoretical concepts you need to know for all the Phases that compose the goal.

A **Phase** is a set of exercises that delve into an area of knowledge within the objective. In each phase, we include the source code along with its explanation; also, we have an example of the source code execution.

The **Projects** are exercises of advanced difficulty that allow consolidating the knowledge acquired in the previous Goals. During the apprenticeship, you develop five Projects:

- **First Project**: Strengthen knowledge of Goals 1 to 4.
- **Second Project**: Strengthen knowledge of Goals 5.
- **Third Project**: Strengthen knowledge of Goals 6.
- **Fourth Project**: Strengthen knowledge of Goals 7 to 9.
- **Final Project**: Strengthen knowledge of all Goals.

The second and fourth project are evolutionary projects of the first project. With them, you are applying new knowledge to the first project for a better understanding of everything you are learning.

## WEEKEND DISTRIBUTION

The learning method has been designed and optimized so that you be able to learn Python in a weekend. Your previous knowledge can slightly modify the learning time.

The recommended learning sequence that you should follow to achieve the goal of learning Python is as follows:

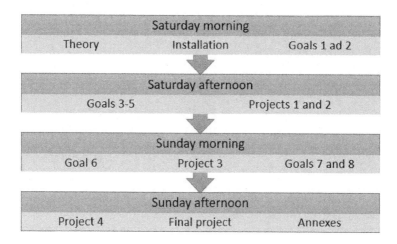

| Saturday morning | | |
| --- | --- | --- |
| Theory | Installation | Goals 1 ad 2 |

| Saturday afternoon | |
| --- | --- |
| Goals 3-5 | Projects 1 and 2 |

| Sunday morning | | |
| --- | --- | --- |
| Goal 6 | Project 3 | Goals 7 and 8 |

| Sunday afternoon | | |
| --- | --- | --- |
| Project 4 | Final project | Annexes |

In this section, we are going to explain a series of not linked to the programming activity previous concepts. They make you have a better understanding of what programming is.

## WHAT IS A PROGRAM?

The first concept you have to understand when you start to learn programming is what a program is. A **program** is a set of instructions or steps to follow that are given to a computer in sequence to perform a specific task.

The normal flow of a program is as follows:

1. The program receives input data, usually entered by its users.
2. The program executes the instructions specified by the programmer.
3. The program outputs a set of output data.

The following image shows what a program would look like from a high-level point of view, that is, what a user sees relative to a program:

## WHAT IS PROGRAMMING?

Once you have understood what a program is, it is time for you to become familiar with the term "programming". It is nothing more than the action of telling a computer exactly what it has to do and how it has to do using a specific programming language.

Programming languages allow programmers to transform their idea of the program into a set of instructions that the computer is capable of executing.

In this section, we explain theoretical concepts about Python and teach you why it is a powerful programming language and why you should learn it.

## WHAT IS PYTHON?

Python is a programming language that was created in the late 80s by the Dutch Guido van Rossum. He was a fan of the humorous group Monty Python, hence the name he gave to the programming language.

The characteristics of the language are as follows:

- **Simplicity**: Python's high strength!

- **Exact syntax**: Python syntax is distinct; it is mandatory to use indentation in all code. Thanks to this feature, all programs are written in Python have the same appearance.

- **General-purpose**: all kinds of programs can be created, including web pages.

- **Interpreted**: a language that is an interpreted means that an interpreter rather than the computer executes it. It means that it is not necessary to compile it (translate it to a specific language that the machine understands). An interpreted language is slower than a non-interpreted language.

- **High-level language**: you don't need to worry about low-level aspects such as the memory management of the program.

- **Object-oriented**: Python bases on the most used paradigm to program nowadays, object-oriented programming.

- **Open Source**: Python has been ported to different operating systems, so you can use it in the one you like. Another characteristic of being Open Source is that it is a free programming language.

- **Extensive libraries**: they facilitate programming by incorporating a large number of functionalities through libraries.

- **Embeddable**: it is possible to add programs written in Python to programs written in other languages, such as C or C ++.

Python is a complete programming language! Of all the features that it has, the key to its great success is the first one, the simplicity, which makes it perfect to start in the world of programming.

## THE ZEN OF PYTHON

Tim Peters wrote a document to embody the philosophy of the Python language. You can find it at https://www.python.org/dev/peps/pep-0020/. Next, you find the Python mantras:

- Beautiful is better than ugly.
- Explicit is better than implicit.
- Simple is better than complex.
- Complex is better than complicated.
- Flat is better than nested.

13

- Sparse is better than dense.
- Readability counts.
- Special cases aren't special enough to break the rules.
- Although practicality beats purity.
- Errors should never pass silently.
- Unless explicitly silenced.
- In the face of ambiguity, refuse the temptation to guess.
- There should be one-- and preferably only one -- obvious way to do it.
- Although that way may not be obvious at first unless you're Dutch.
- Now is better than never.
- Although never is often better than *right* now.
- If the implementation is hard to explain, it's a bad idea.
- If the implementation is easy to explain, it may be a good idea.
- Namespaces are one great honking idea -- let's do more of those!

## WHY PYTHON?

Currently, many programming languages are very similar to each other (Java, C#, C++, others). The only thing that changes between them is the syntax used to program. The syntax is an excellent thing, since learning one of these languages do not cost you to learn another of them. You only have to learn the specific syntax of the language you want to learn.

In this section, we are going to explain the reasons why you should learn Python. These reasons are valid whether you are new to programming or not. When you finish reading the section, we are sure that your opinion is that Python is the perfect language to learn to program.

There are many reasons why you should learn to program in Python. Let's see the most important:

**Simplicity**

The main characteristic of Python is that it is a simple language; it considerably reduces the number of lines of code compared to other languages. It provides tools to perform operations more straightforwardly than with other languages.

Let's see an example with the typical first program that is usually done with all programming languages when you start learning them, the *"Hello World"*.

The program in the Java programming language would be the following:

```
1  package example;
2
3  public class example {
4
5  public static void main(String[] args) {
6      System.out.print("Hello Time of Software");
7  }
8
9  }
```

The Python program would be the following:

```
print("Hello Time of Software")
```

Thanks to the simplicity of Python, the errors that a programmer can make when making programs are lower since having to write less source code reduce the probability of making errors. Also, a significant point related to simplicity is that by writing fewer lines of code, development time decreases. Time is something vital to take into account when carrying out software development projects.

What do you think? Python is very straightforward and simple compared to all other languages!

## Quick results

When you are learning to program, you like to see results of what you are learning. With Python, you can see the results immediately.

Python allows you to be making programs within a few days (even hours) of starting. You see that you progress almost effortlessly at high speed.

## Starting Point

Python is a complete language. Please, do not think that it is not complete due it is simple. With Python, you learn all the existing concepts in the world of programming, such as object-oriented programming (OOP), threads... Python covers all the existing fields within programming.

## Libraries & Modules

Python is a powerful language. As you become familiar with the language and learn and handle all the functionalities, you discover that Python has a pervasive set of libraries and modules. These libraries and modules allow you to carry out any type of project, regardless of its nature.

## Web development

Many frameworks use Python for web development; among them, Django stands out. As you can see, the mantra that heads its web page is the same as Python:

*Django makes it easier to build better Web apps more quickly and with less code.*

In Django Sites, you can find many web pages made with Django.

## Raspberry Pi

Python is Raspberry's primary programming language.

## Community

The community behind this programming language is immense, which means that the language is not obsolete and is receiving updates. Another strong point of the community behind it is the creation of frameworks, modules, extensions and a multitude of tools that facilitate development with this language. Python developers are the first interested in having more people programming with Python, since, in this way, the number of tools/frameworks that facilitate development be more significant.

One of the most important things for someone starting with a programming language is the help that the community that surrounds the programming language offers. If you dare to learn Python, you see how you can easily find the resolution of your questions/doubts/problems.

Programming in Python never feels lonely!

## High labour demand

The world's great technology companies use Python. Knowing Python means having a better chance of finding that job you have always wanted to have.

Python has a development environment called IDLE (**I**ntegrated **D**eve**L**opment **E**nvironment or **I**ntegrated **D**evelopment and **L**earning **E**nvironment). Python includes the development environment since version 1.5. The intention is to be used as a learning environment thanks to its simplicity.

As we have commented in the previous point, the name of Python honours the Monty Python, comic group. The name for the development environment, IDLE, could have been chosen by the last name of one of its founding members, Eric Idle.

To install Python, you have to navigate to https://www.python.org.

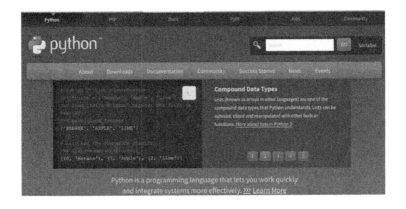

Once you are inside the Python website, you have to navigate to the *Downloads* section. By default, you get to download the version that corresponds to the operating system of your computer. The version we use is 3.8.

## INSTALLATION

In the following points, we explain how to install Python on the most popular operating systems:

- Mac OS X
- Microsoft Windows
- Linux

## MAC OS X INSTALLATION

To install Python on Mac OS X, once you download the file you have to execute it, and the installer's home screen appears:

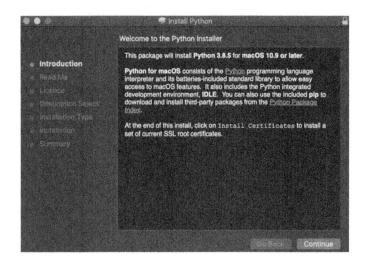

To start installing, you have to accept the terms of the Python software license agreement:

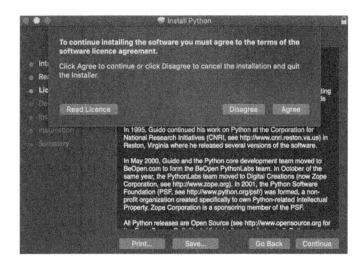

The next step is to select the hard drive where you are going to install Python:

The installer asks you for the password of the administrator user to continue with the installation:

The installer completes the installation after granting it all administrator permission that it needs:

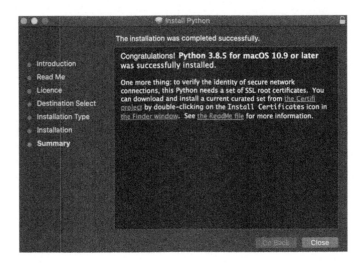

After completing the installation, the Python IDLE is available to use in the launchpad:

IDLE          Python Launcher

## MICROSOFT WINDOWS INSTALLATION

To install Python on Microsoft Windows, you have to execute the downloaded installer. In the first screen of the installer, you can select the installation path, install for all users and add Python to the system path.

Once you have everything selected and you set the installation path, you have to press "*Install Now*":

The installation process finishes:

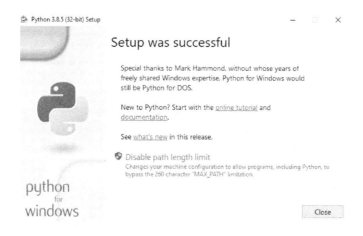

Access to Python IDLE is within the start menu.

## LINUX INSTALLATION

After downloading the Python file, you have to navigate using the *Terminal* to the folder where you have saved it and execute the following command "*tar xvf Python-3.8.5.tar.xz*":

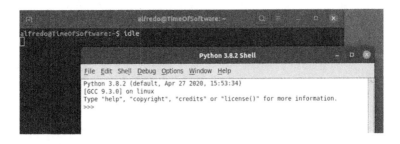

Once the previous command executes, it is time to install Python, for this, you enter the folder that the previous command has created, and you execute the command "*./configure*":

Now you have Python installed. It is time to install IDLE. To do this, use the following command, and it installs it automatically:

To execute IDLE, it is as simple as opening the *Terminal* and executing the "*idle*" command:

# GETTING FAMILIAR WITH THE DEVELOPMENT ENVIRONMENT

This section explains the development environment with which you carry out all the objectives, phases and projects that we propose in this book.

When you open the development environment, you find an image like the following:

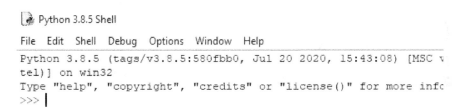

To create a new Python file and write a program, you have to enter the *"File / New File"* menu. It opens a new screen where you write the source code of your programs.

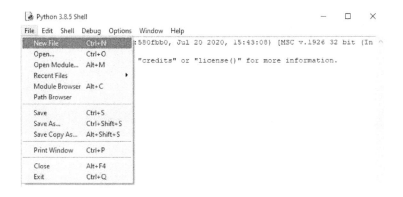

Once you write the source code of the program, you have to save it from being able to run it. To run the program, you have to go to the *"Run / Run Module"* menu, and the program executes.

The process that you have just done creating a file and executing it is what you must do in each exercise that we propose in the book. Therefore, for each exercise, you must do the following steps:

1. Create a new file.
2. Write the source code.
3. Save the file.
4. Run the program.

As you use IDLE, you notice that IDLE uses different colours to highlight different reserved words and different messages that display in the console and the code editor. The colours it uses are the following:

- Orange: Python reserved words.
- Green: text strings.
- Blue: the result of the execution of a sentence.
- Red: error messages.
- Purple: functions.

In this first objective, you learn to manage the input and output of information through the screen.

Displaying information on the screen and reading user information are necessary operations to achieve high interactivity with the applications that you develop and their users.

The objective is composed of two phases. In the first, you learn how to show information to users, and in the second, you learn to read information from users.

## THEORETICAL CONCEPTS

In this section, we explain the two commands with which you start programming in Python.

## PRINT

The *print* command allows you to display information on the screen to the user of the application. The command can be used with multiple text strings to be displayed at once, separated by commas. In this way, it simplifies not having to write a sentence for each message that we want to display sequentially on the screen, and it inserts a blank space between the different strings.

The command is as follow:

*print(TextString1, TextString2, TextStringN)*

The content of *TextStrings* displays on the screen.

You can use the following parameters with the *print* command:

- **end**: allows adding a text string as the final element of the set of text strings that display on the screen.

- **sep**: allows adding a text string to the end of each string sent to display on the screen. Also, it replaces the blank space that is entered by default between the different text strings to display on the screen.

The command with parameters is as follow:

*print(TextString1, TextStringN, end="TextStringEnd",
sep="TextStringSep")*

The content of the different text strings use for:
- *TextStrings:* they show on the screen.
- *TextStringEnd:* text that adds to the final element of the text strings.
- *TextStringSep:* text string added to the end of all text string.

---

## INPUT

The *input* command allows you to read information entered by the users of the application through the keyboard.

The command returns the text entered by the users as a simple text string. In the case of needing a different type of data, you have to transform the text string to the type of data you need (we explain it later).

The command is as follow:

$$TextReaded = input()$$

*TextReaded* is where the introduced text stores. The application user must press the *Enter* key to read the text entered by the application.

## VARIABLES

Variables are data that you need to store and use in programs and that reside in the computer's memory. They have the following characteristics:

- **Name**: identifier within the source code that we use to use them.
- **Type**: type of data that the variable stores.
- **Value**: value that they store. When declaring a variable, you have to indicate an initial value, which can be modified as the program runs.

An example of the use of variables can be the need to store the user's age in your program. To do this, you would create a variable with a specific name and the type of data that you would store in. It would be an integer.

In Python, the names of the variables follow these rules:
- Letters from A to Z, both in uppercase and lowercase.
- Numbers from 0 to 9 (except for the first character of the name).
- It can contain the "_" character.

The Python language has reserved words that you cannot use as variable names. In the annexes of the book, you can find the list of Python reserved words and the use of all of them.

Here are some examples of variables in Python:

- age = 4
- name = "Alfredo"

The first variable, *age*, stores the numeric value 4, while the second variable, *name*, stores the text string "Alfredo".

As you can see, in Python, the data type is not established when declaring a variable. There is no declaration itself as it exists in other languages; you simply write the name you want it to have and assign the corresponding value.

## PHASE 1: DISPLAY INFORMATION ON THE SCREEN

The first phase of this objective consists of learning how to use the *print* command through a series of exercises that allow you to display information on the screen to users.

The first exercise in the phase consists of displaying a couple of messages on the screen in a simple way. The source code is as follows:

```
print("Hello Time of Software!")
print("This is my first program with Python")
```

The execution of the above source code has the following output:

```
================== RESTART: /Users/alfre/Desktop/Python/1-1-1.py ==================
Hello Time of Software!
This is my first program with Python
>>>
```

The second exercise in the phase consists of using the *sep* parameter when you use the print command. The source code is as follows:

```
print(1,2,3,4,5)
print(1,2,3,4,5, sep=',')
```

The execution of the above source code has the following output:

```
================= RESTART: /Users/alfre/Desktop/Python/1-1-2.py =================
1 2 3 4 5
1,2,3,4,5
>>>
```

The third exercise in the phase consists of the use of the *end* parameter when you use the print command. The source code is as follows:

```
print(1,2,3,4,5, sep=',', end='.')
```

The execution of the above source code has the following output:

```
================= RESTART: /Users/alfre/Desktop/Python/1-1-3.py =================
1,2,3,4,5.
>>>
```

# PHASE 2: READ INFORMATION FROM THE KEYBOARD

The second phase of this objective consists of learning the *input* command through a series of exercises that allow you to read the information entered by the application users.

The first exercise in the phase consists of reading the name of the user application and show it on the screen. The exercise uses the variable "*name*" to store the user's name information and then display it on the screen in the next instruction. The source code is as follows:

31

```
print("Hello! We are Time of Software, What is your name?")
name = input()
print("Thank you very much to choose us to learn Python, ", name)
```

The execution of the above source code has the following output:

```
================= RESTART: /Users/alfre/Desktop/Python/1-2-1.py =================
Hello! We are Time of Software, What is your name?
Alfredo
Thank you very much to choose us to learn Python,  Alfredo
>>>
```

The second exercise in the phase consists of using the *input* command with a text as a parameter. The text is displayed, and later the application waits for the user to enter the text. The exercise uses the variable "*age*" to store the age of the user and later display it on the screen in the next instruction. The source code is as follows:

```
age = input("How old are you?: ")
print("You are",age,"years old.")
```

The execution of the above source code has the following output:

```
================= RESTART: /Users/alfre/Desktop/Python/1-2-2.py =================
How old are you?: 36
You are 36 years old.
>>>
```

## NOW YOU CAN...

In this first objective, you have learned the following knowledge:

- Show information on the screen.
- Read information entered by the users of the applications through the keyboard.
- Use of variables.

In this second objective, you learn the different types of data that exist in Python and how to use them.

The objective contains five phases with the content as follows:
- The first phase: you learn to use numbers and the different arithmetic operations.
- The second phase: you learn to use text strings fundamentals.
- The third phase: you learn to use different data collections.
- The fourth phase: you learn the Boolean data type and the different logical operations.
- Fifth phase: you learn to use text strings in an advanced way.

## THEORETICAL CONCEPTS

In this section, we are going to explain the different types of data that exist in Python and the different operations that you can perform with the data.

## DATA TYPES

In computing, information is nothing more than a sequence of zeros and ones that are structured in blocks to facilitate its handling.

Therefore, the type of information (the type of data) typifies all the information that exists. A text string is not the same as an integer or float number.

Variables in Python can be of the following types:

| Datatype | Description |
|---|---|
| Numbers | Numbers can be of the following types:<br>• int (signed integers)<br>• long (long integers)<br>• float (floating point real values)<br>• complex (complex numbers) |
| Strings | Text. |
| Booleans | They can have two values: True or False |
| List | They are composed of an array of elements that can be of different types of data. |
| Tuples | Immutable list of elements. |
| Dictionary | List of elements that contain keys and values. |

Variables do not have a specific type in Python. You can use a variable to store a number in a part of your program, and later you can use it to store a list of elements.

## OPERATORS

Python has different operators that also exist in other programming languages, and they can be grouped based on the function they perform:

- Assignment operators.
- Arithmetic operators.
- Relational operators.
- Logical operators.

## ASSIGNMENT OPERATOR

Although we have already used it in objective number 1, the assignment operator '=' is used to assign a value to a variable. Whatever is on the right side of the operator is assigned (stored) in the variable on the left side. Let's see some examples:

34

- price = 923
- surname = "Moreno"
- number = 34

In the first example, *price* contains the value *923*. *Surname* contains *"Moreno"* in the second example. Finally, *number* contains the value *34*.

## ARITHMETIC OPERATORS

Arithmetic operators are those operators that allow us to perform arithmetic operations with the data.

A good practice when using arithmetic operators is to use parentheses to establish the specific order of resolution of operations. The reason is that each programming language establishes the resolution differently, and you can find erroneous results. Let's see some examples:

- multiplicationresult = 8 * 4
- cost = (6*11)-4
- dollars = 50/4

In the first example, *multiplicationresult* contains the multiplication result. *Cost* contains the operation result in the second example. Finally, *dollars* contain the division result.

## RELATIONAL OPERATORS

Relational operators are those that allow you to make comparisons between two elements. They are as follows:

| Operator | Meaning |
| --- | --- |
| < | Less than |
| > | Greater than |
| <= | Less than or equal to |
| > = | Greater than or equal to |
| == | Like |
| ! = | Other than |

The result of a relational operation can only be two values:

- **true**: the comparison is satisfied.
- **false**: the comparison is not satisfied.

Let's see some examples:

- 7 <5
- 9 == 3
- 2 <12
- 88> = 4

In the first example, the check returns *false*, in the second it returns *false*, in the third, it returns *true*, and in the fourth, it returns *true*.

## LOGICAL OPERATORS

The logical operators allow you to combine the relational operation result values or independent *Boolean* values to obtain a single result. The logical operators that you can use are the following:

- **AND**: logical operator that performs the logical *'AND'* operation between two elements. The result is *true* if both elements are *true*. Otherwise, it is *false*.

- **OR**: logical operator that performs the *'OR'* logical operation between two elements. The result is *true* if one of the two elements is *true*. Otherwise, it is *false*.
- **NOT**: logical operator that performs the logical *'NOT'* operation. The result is *true* if the element is *false*, and it is *false* if the element is *true*.

The logical operators can be used in combined expressions, for this, as we have explained in the arithmetic operators, we advise you to use parentheses to separate the different expressions.

Let's see some examples:

- (5 <3) AND (4 == 7)
- (1 <7) OR (3 == 3)
- NOT (6 == 7)
- True AND False

In the first example, the check returns the value *false*; in the second, it returns the value *true*; in the third, it returns the value *true* and in the fourth *false*.

## PHASE 1: NUMBERS AND ARITHMETIC OPERATORS

The first phase of this objective consists of learning the use of numbers and arithmetic operations. The phase contains as many groups as the different arithmetic operators. Finally, the phase has a section to learn how to round real numbers.

You have to keep in mind that the word *int* specifies the integer numbers and *float* specifies the real ones. In the different exercises, you are going to transform what the user enters with the *input* command to integers or real numbers to perform the different arithmetical operations. To transform the values, you have to do it in the following way:

- **Integer number**: int(input("text")).
- **Real number**: float(input("text")).

You have to assign the result to a variable to be able to use it later.

## SUM

The first exercise of the phase consists of carrying out a sum of two integers numbers entered by the user. The source code is as follows:

```
sumand1 = int(input("Enter the first summand (integer): "))
sumand2 = int(input("Enter the second summand (integer): "))
print("Result: ", sumand1 + sumand2)
```

The execution of the above source code has the following output:

```
================= RESTART: /Users/alfre/Desktop/Python/2-1-1.py ================
Enter the first summand (integer): 52
Enter the second summand (integer): 86
Result:  138
>>>
```

The second exercise of the phase consists of carrying out a sum of two real numbers entered by the user. The source code is as follows:

```
sumand1 = float(input("Enter the first summand (float): "))
sumand2 = float(input("Enter the second summand (float): "))
print("Result: ", sumand1 + sumand2)
```

The execution of the above source code has the following output:

```
================= RESTART: /Users/alfre/Desktop/Python/2-1-2.py ================
Enter the first summand (float): 27.35
Enter the second summand (float): 54.12
Result:  81.47
>>>
```

## SUBTRACTION

The third exercise of the phase consists of carrying out a subtraction of two integers numbers entered by the user. The source code is as follows:

minuend = int(input("Enter the minuend (integer): "))
subtrahend = int(input("Enter the subtrahend (integer): "))
print("Result: ", minuend - subtrahend)

The execution of the above source code has the following output:

```
================= RESTART: /Users/alfre/Desktop/Python/2-1-3.py =================
Enter the  minuend (integer): 76
Enter the subtrahend (integer): 23
Result:  53
>>>
```

The fourth exercise in the phase consists of a subtracting two real numbers entered by the user. The source code is as follows:

minuend = float(input("Enter the minuend (float): "))
subtrahend = float(input("Enter the subtrahend (float): "))
print("Result: ", minuend - subtrahend)

The execution of the above source code has the following output:

```
================= RESTART: /Users/alfre/Desktop/Python/2-1-4.py =================
Enter the minuend (float): 63.23
Enter the subtrahend (float): 49.67
Result:  13.559999999999995
>>>
```

## MULTIPLICATION

The fifth exercise of the phase consists of carrying out a multiplication of two integers numbers entered by the user. The source code is as follows:

39

```
multiplicand = int(input("Enter the multiplicand (integer): "))
multiplier = int(input("Enter the multiplier (integer): "))
print("Result: ", multiplicand * multiplier)
```

The execution of the above source code has the following output:

```
================= RESTART: /Users/alfre/Desktop/Python/2-1-5.py =================
Enter the multiplicand (integer): 83
Enter the multiplier (integer): 5
Result:   415
>>>
```

The sixth exercise of the phase consists of carrying out a multiplication of two real numbers entered by the user. The source code is as follows:

```
multiplicand = float(input("Enter the multiplicand (float): "))
multiplier = float(input("Enter the multiplier (float): "))
print("Result: ", multiplicand * multiplier)
```

The execution of the above source code has the following output:

```
================= RESTART: /Users/alfre/Desktop/Python/2-1-6.py =================
Enter the multiplicand (float): 34.98
Enter the multiplier (float): 2.3
Result:   80.454
>>>
```

## DIVISION

The seventh exercise of the phase consists of carrying out a division of two integers numbers entered by the user. The source code is as follows:

```
dividend = int(input("Enter the dividend (integer): "))
divider = int(input("Enter the divider (integer): "))
print("Result: ", dividend / divider)
```

The execution of the above source code has the following output:

```
================= RESTART: /Users/alfre/Desktop/Python/2-1-7.py =================
Enter the dividend (integer): 65
Enter the divider (integer): 4
Result:  16.25
>>>
```

The eighth exercise of the phase consists of carrying out a division of two real numbers entered by the user. The source code is as follows:

```
dividend = float(input("Enter the dividend (float): "))
divider = float(input("Enter the divider (float): "))
print("Result: ", dividend / divider)
```

The execution of the above source code has the following output:

```
================= RESTART: /Users/alfre/Desktop/Python/2-1-8.py =================
Enter the dividend (float): 34.64
Enter the divider (float): 7.89
Result:  4.3776932826362485
>>>
```

## ROUNDING OF REAL NUMBERS

In this exercise, you learn how to round real numbers using the *round* instruction.

The *round* instruction uses two parameters to execute. The first one is the real number you want to round and the second one is the number of decimal digits you want to have with the rounding.

The ninth exercise of the phase consists of rounding the result of the division to a real number with only one decimal digit. The source code is as follows:

```
dividend = float(input("Enter the dividend (float): "))
divider = float(input("Enter the divider (float): "))
result = round(dividend / divider,1)
print("Result: ", result)
```

41

The execution of the above source code has the following output:

```
================ RESTART: /Users/alfre/Desktop/Python/2-1-9.py ================
Enter the dividend (float): 76.9
Enter the divider (float): 33.1
Result:   2.3
>>>
```

## PHASE 2: TEXT STRINGS (BASIC)

The second phase of this objective consists of learning the use of text strings.

The first exercise of the phase consists of storing a text string in a variable and displaying it on the screen. The source code is as follows.

```
examplestring = "Hello Time of Software"
print(examplestring)
```

The execution of the above source code has the following output:

```
================ RESTART: /Users/alfre/Desktop/Python/2-2-1.py ================
Hello Time of Software
>>>
```

The second exercise of the phase is the same as the previous one. Still, with this exercise, you learn to introduce special characters (or escape characters) in text strings. In the exercise, you are going to introduce the character '\n', which implies a line break within the text string. The source code is as follows:

```
examplestring = "Hello Time of Software\nThis is a multilinea\nstring"
print(examplestring)
```

The execution of the above source code has the following output:

```
================ RESTART: /Users/alfre/Desktop/Python/2-2-2.py ================
Hello Time of Software
This is a multilinea
string
>>>
```

There are various special characters for text strings. You can find a description of all of them in the annexe at the end of the book.

## PHASE 3: COLLECTIONS

The third phase of this objective consists of learning and using the different collections that are available in Python. The collections that we are going to learn are the following:

- Lists.
- Tuples.
- Dictionaries.

## LISTS

A list is an ordered set of items that can contain data of any type. It is the most flexible type of collection in Python. Lists can contain items of the same type or items of different types.

In Python, lists are delimited with square brackets "[ ]", with items separated by **commas**.

The first exercise in the phase consists of storing a list in a variable and displaying it on the screen. The source code is as follows:

```
itemlist = ["computer","keyboard","mouse"]
print(itemlist)
```

The execution of the above source code has the following output:

```
================= RESTART: /Users/alfre/Desktop/Python/2-3-1.py =================
['computer', 'keyboard', 'mouse']
>>>
```

The second exercise in the phase consists of storing a list in a variable, calculating the number of elements using the *len* instruction, and displaying the elements of the list individually on the screen. **Note that the first element of a list is element 0, not 1.**

To access the list elements, you have to use the **name of the variable** followed by **square brackets** and the **position** in the list you want to access. For example, if you want to access the element number 2 of a list called *itemlist,* you have to do in this way:

*itemlist[2]*

The source code of the exercise is as follows:

```
itemlist = ["computer","keyboard","mouse"]
print(len(itemlist))
print(itemlist[0])
print(itemlist[1])
print(itemlist[2])
```

The execution of the above source code has the following output:

```
================= RESTART: /Users/alfre/Desktop/Python/2-3-2.py =================
3
computer
keyboard
mouse
>>>
```

The third exercise of the phase consists of the union of two lists previously created using the arithmetic operator '+' and its storage in a new variable. The screen shows the result of the union of the two lists. The source code is as follows:

```
originallist = ["computer","keyboard","mouse"]
newlist = ["screen","printer","speakers"]
finallist = originallist + newlist
print(finallist)
```

The execution of the above source code has the following output:

```
================ RESTART: /Users/alfre/Desktop/Python/2-3-3.py ================
['computer', 'keyboard', 'mouse', 'screen', 'printer', 'speakers']
>>>
```

The fourth exercise of the phase consists of adding an element to a list using the arithmetic operator '+'. The screen shows the list twice to check the assignment: the original list at the beginning and the resulting list after adding the element. The source code is as follows:

```
itemlist = ["computer","keyboard","mouse"]
print(itemlist)
itemlist = itemlist + ["table"]
print(itemlist)
```

The execution of the above source code has the following output:

```
================ RESTART: /Users/alfre/Desktop/Python/2-3-4.py ================
['computer', 'keyboard', 'mouse']
['computer', 'keyboard', 'mouse', 'table']
>>>
```

The fifth exercise of the phase consists of modifying the values of the elements of a list using the assignment operator. The screen shows the list twice to check the modification: the initial list at the beginning and the one resulting from the modifications of the values. The source code is as follows:

```
itemlist = ["computer","keyboard","mouse"]
print(itemlist)
itemlist[0] = "screen"
itemlist[1] = "printer"
itemlist[2] = "speakers"
print(itemlist)
```

The execution of the above source code has the following output:

```
================ RESTART: /Users/alfre/Desktop/Python/2-3-5.py ================
['computer', 'keyboard', 'mouse']
['screen', 'printer', 'speakers']
>>>
```

The sixth exercise of the phase consists of removing an element from the list using the *del* instruction. The screen shows twice the list to check the deletion: the initial list at the beginning and the resulting list after deleting the element. The source code is as follows:

```
itemlist = ["computer","keyboard","mouse"]
print(itemlist)
del itemlist[1]
print(itemlist)
```

The execution of the above source code has the following output:

```
================= RESTART: /Users/alfre/Desktop/Python/2-3-6.py =================
['computer', 'keyboard', 'mouse']
['computer', 'mouse']
>>>
```

The seventh exercise in the phase consists of creating lists as list elements. The exercise creates a list consisting of three text strings and an item list that contains text strings. As we told you in the explanation of list data types, the elements of a list do not have to be of the same type. In this case, we are creating a list that contains text strings and another list as elements. The exercise shows all main list elements and later, the elements of the list defined within the main list. The source code is as follows:

```
itemlist = ["computer","keyboard","mouse", ["soundcard","microphone","speakers"]]
print(itemlist[0])
print(itemlist[1])
print(itemlist[2])
print(itemlist[3])
print(itemlist[3][0])
print(itemlist[3][1])
print(itemlist[3][2])
```

The execution of the above source code has the following output:

```
================= RESTART: /Users/alfre/Desktop/Python/2-3-7.py =================
computer
keyboard
mouse
['soundcard', 'microphone', 'speakers']
soundcard
microphone
speakers
>>>
```

## TUPLES

Tuples are a set of ordered and immutable elements. The difference with lists is that in lists, you can manipulate the elements, and in tuples, you cannot. Tuples can contain elements of the same type or elements of different types, just like lists.

In Python, tuples are delimited by **parentheses "( )"**, with the elements separated by **commas**.

The eighth exercise of the phase consists of creating a tuple of elements and storing it in a variable. The screen shows the elements of the tuple together, the number of elements that make up the tuple and each element independently. **Note that, as in lists, the first element of the tuples is 0, not 1**. The source code is as follows:

```
itemtuple = ("computer","keyboard","mouse")
print(itemtuple)
print(len(itemtuple))
print(itemtuple[0])
print(itemtuple[1])
print(itemtuple[2])
```

The execution of the above source code has the following output:

```
================= RESTART: /Users/alfre/Desktop/Python/2-3-8.py =================
('computer', 'keyboard', 'mouse')
3
computer
keyboard
mouse
>>>
```

# DICTIONARIES

Dictionaries are collections of items made up of a key and an associated value. Dictionaries do not allow to have duplicate keys so that you cannot repeat them.

In Python, dictionaries are delimited with **brackets** "{ }", with items separated by **commas** and the key separated from the value by a **colon**.

The ninth exercise of the phase consists of creating a dictionary with the months of the year and storing them in a variable. The key of the dictionary elements will be the name of the month in English and the value is the name of the month in Spanish. Subsequently, a couple of dictionary elements are accessed using the key in English and the value in Spanish is displayed on the screen. The source code is as follows:

```
translatedmonths = {"January" : "Enero",
            "February" : "Febrero",
            "March" : "Marzo",
            "April" : "Abril",
            "May" : "Mayo",
            "June" : "Junio",
            "July" : "Julio",
            "August" : "Agosto",
            "September" : "Septiembre",
            "October" : "Octubre",
            "November" : "Noviembre",
            "December" : "Diciembre"}
print(translatedmonths["November"])
print(translatedmonths["May"])
```

The execution of the above source code has the following output:

```
================= RESTART: /Users/alfre/Desktop/Python/2-3-9.py =================
Noviembre
Mayo
>>>
```

# PHASE 4: BOOLEANS AND LOGICAL AND RELATIONAL OPERATORS

The fourth phase of this objective consists of learning the use of boolean data types and the use of logical and relational operators.

## BOOLEANS

A boolean variable is a variable that can only take two possible values: *True* (true or 1) or *False* (false or 0).

The first exercise in the phase consists of storing the value *True* in a variable and displaying it on the screen. Note that the value *True* is entered as such, not as a text string since these values (*True* and *False*) are part of the Python programming language. The source code is as follows:

```
boolean = True
print(boolean)
```

The execution of the above source code has the following output:

```
================= RESTART: /Users/alfre/Desktop/Python/2-4-1.py =================
True
>>>
```

The second exercise in the phase consists of storing the value *False* in a variable and displaying it on the screen. The source code is as follows:

```
boolean = False
print(boolean)
```

The execution of the above source code has the following output:

49

## LOGICAL OPERATORS

Logical operators are operations that can be performed on boolean variables, whether they are independent values or values from other relational operations.

The third exercise of the phase consists of performing an *AND* operation on two *True* values. The screen displays the result of the operation. The source code is as follows:

```
boolean1 = True
boolean2 = True
print(boolean1 and boolean2)
```

The execution of the above source code has the following output:

```
=============== RESTART: /Users/alfre/Desktop/Python/2-4-3.py ===============
True
>>>
```

The fourth exercise of the phase consists of carrying out an *AND* operation on a *True* and a *False* value. The screen displays the result of the operation. The source code is as follows:

```
boolean1 = True
boolean2 = False
print(boolean1 and boolean2)
```

The execution of the above source code has the following output:

```
=============== RESTART: /Users/alfre/Desktop/Python/2-4-4.py ===============
False
>>>
```

The fifth exercise of the phase consists of performing an *AND* operation on two *False* values. The screen displays the result of the operation. The source code is as follows:

```
boolean1 = False
boolean2 = False
print(boolean1 and boolean2)
```

The execution of the above source code has the following output:

```
================= RESTART: /Users/alfre/Desktop/Python/2-4-5.py =================
False
>>>
```

At this point, you have been able to practice the different possibilities of operations allowed with booleans and the *AND* operator. Now you do the same with the *OR* operator.

The sixth exercise of the phase consists of performing an *OR* operation on two *True* values. The screen displays the result of the operation. The source code is as follows:

```
boolean1 = True
boolean2 = True
print(boolean1 or boolean2)
```

The execution of the above source code has the following output:

```
================= RESTART: /Users/alfre/Desktop/Python/2-4-6.py =================
True
>>>
```

The seventh exercise of the phase consists of performing an *OR* operation on a *True* and *False* value. The screen displays the result of the operation. The source code is as follows:

```
boolean1 = True
boolean2 = False
print(boolean1 or boolean2)
```

The execution of the above source code has the following output:

```
================ RESTART: /Users/alfre/Desktop/Python/2-4-7.py ================
True
>>>
```

The eighth exercise of the phase consists of performing an *OR* operation on two *False* values. The screen displays the result of the operation. The source code is as follows:

```
boolean1 = False
boolean2 = False
print(boolean1 or boolean2)
```

The execution of the above source code has the following output:

```
================ RESTART: /Users/alfre/Desktop/Python/2-4-8.py ================
False
>>>
```

The ninth exercise consists of the use of the logical *NOT* operator with the value *False*. The screen displays the result of the operation. The source code is as follows:

```
boolean = False
print(not boolean)
```

The execution of the above source code has the following output:

```
================ RESTART: /Users/alfre/Desktop/Python/2-4-9.py ================
True
>>>
```

The tenth exercise of the phase consists of the use of the logical *NOT* operator with the value *True*. The screen displays the result of the operation. The source code is as follows:

```
boolean = True
print(not boolean)
```

The execution of the above source code has the following output:

As we indicated in the theoretical part of the objective, we recommend using parentheses when doing complex logical operations. When composing more complicated expressions, keep in mind that Python evaluates *NOTs* first, then *ANDs*, and lastly *ORs*.

## RELATIONAL OPERATORS

Relational operators are comparison operations that you can use on data, either directly or through the use of variables.

The eleventh exercise consists of performing all the relational operations with the values stored by the variables *number1* and *number2*. The screen shows the result of all operations. The source code is as follows.

```
number1 = 6
number2 = 9
print(number1 > number2)
print(number1 >= number2)
print(number1 < number2)
print(number1 <= number2)
print(number1 == number2)
print(number1 != number2)
```

The execution of the above source code has the following output:

```
=============== RESTART: /Users/alfre/Desktop/Python/2-4-11.py ================
False
False
True
True
False
True
>>>
```

53

## PHASE 5: TEXT STRINGS (ADVANCED)

The fifth phase of this objective consists of learning advanced commands that are very useful for working with text strings.

The first exercise of the phase consists of learning the *capitalize* instruction, which allows you to put the first letter of a text string in uppercase. The screen displays the result of the operation. The source code is as follows:

```
examplestring = "in a galaxy far away..."
print(examplestring.capitalize())
```

The execution of the above source code has the following output:

```
================== RESTART: /Users/alfre/Desktop/Python/2-5-1.py ================
In a galaxy far away...
>>>
```

The second exercise of the phase consists of learning the *upper* instruction, which allows you to capitalize a text string completely. The screen displays the result of the operation. The source code is as follows:

```
examplestring = "in a galaxy far away..."
print(examplestring.upper())
```

The execution of the above source code has the following output:

```
================== RESTART: /Users/alfre/Desktop/Python/2-5-2.py ================
IN A GALAXY FAR AWAY...
>>>
```

The third exercise in the phase consists of learning the *lower* instruction, which does the opposite of the instruction in the previous exercise; it completely lowers a text string. The screen displays the result of the operation. The source code is as follows:

```
examplestring = "IN A GALAXY FAR AWAY..."
print(examplestring.lower())
```

The execution of the above source code has the following output:

```
================= RESTART: /Users/alfre/Desktop/Python/2-5-3.py =================
in a galaxy far away...
>>>
```

The fourth exercise of the phase consists of learning the *len* instruction, which allows you to know the number of characters that make up the text string. The screen displays the result of the operation. The source code is as follows:

```
examplestring = "In a galaxy far away..."
print(len(examplestring))
```

The execution of the above source code has the following output:

```
================= RESTART: /Users/alfre/Desktop/Python/2-5-4.py =================
23
>>>
```

The fifth exercise of the phase consists of learning the *isalnum* instruction, which checks whether all the characters that make up the text string are alphanumeric or not. In the exercise, we check four different text strings and the screen displays the result of the operation. The source code is as follows:

```
examplestring = "In a galaxy far away..."
print(examplestring.isalnum())
examplestring = "1234567890"
print(examplestring.isalnum())
examplestring = "abcdefg1234567890"
print(examplestring.isalnum())
examplestring = "abcdefg 1234567890"
print(examplestring.isalnum())
```

The execution of the above source code has the following output:

```
================ RESTART: /Users/alfre/Desktop/Python/2-5-5.py ================
False
True
True
False
>>>
```

The first and the fourth strings contain non-alphanumeric characters, so those values are *False*. They contain whitespaces.

The sixth exercise of the phase consists of learning the *isalpha* instruction, which checks whether all the characters in the text string are alphabetic or not. In the exercise, we check four different text strings and the screen displays the result of the operation. The source code is as follows:

```
examplestring = "Inagalaxyfaraway"
print(examplestring.isalpha())
examplestring = "In a galaxy far away"
print(examplestring.isalpha())
examplestring = "1234567890"
print(examplestring.isalpha())
examplestring = "abcdefg 1234567890"
print(examplestring.isalpha())
```

The execution of the above source code has the following output:

```
================ RESTART: /Users/alfre/Desktop/Python/2-5-6.py ================
True
False
False
False
>>>
```

As you can see, neither the numbers nor the blank spaces are alphabetic characters. Only the letters make up the set of alphabetic characters.

The seventh exercise of the phase consists of learning the *isdigit* instruction, which checks whether all the characters in the text string are numeric or not. The exercise checks three different text strings. The screen displays the result of the operation. The source code is as follows:

```
examplestring = "In a galaxy far away"
print(examplestring.isdigit())
examplestring = "1234567890"
print(examplestring.isdigit())
examplestring = "abcdefg 1234567890"
print(examplestring.isdigit())
```

The execution of the above source code has the following output:

```
================= RESTART: /Users/alfre/Desktop/Python/2-5-7.py =================
False
True
False
>>>
```

The eighth exercise of the phase consists of learning the *islower* instruction, which checks whether all the characters that make up the string are in lowercase or not. The exercise checks two different text strings. The screen displays the result of the operations. The source code is as follows:

```
examplestring = "In a galaxy far away"
print(examplestring.islower())
examplestring = "in a galaxy far away"
print(examplestring.islower())
```

The execution of the above source code has the following output:

```
================= RESTART: /Users/alfre/Desktop/Python/2-5-8.py =================
False
True
>>>
```

The ninth exercise of the phase consists of learning the *isupper* statement, which checks whether all the characters that make up the text string are uppercase or not. The exercise checks two different text strings. The screen displays the result of the operation. The source code is as follows:

```
examplestring = "In a galaxy far away"
print(examplestring.isupper())
```

57

```
examplestring = "IN A GALAXY FAR AWAY"
print(examplestring.isupper())
```

The execution of the above source code has the following output:

```
================ RESTART: /Users/alfre/Desktop/Python/2-5-9.py ================
False
True
>>>
```

The tenth exercise of the phase consists of learning the instructions *lstrip*, *rstrip* and *strip*, which allow you to eliminate white spaces at the beginning and the end of the text string. To remove the characters from the beginning of the string, you have to use *lstrip*, to remove the characters from the end of the string, you have to use *rstrip*. To remove both at the same time you have to use *strip*, which does the same thing as both but in a single instruction. The exercise executes the instructions with a text string. The screen displays the result of the operation. The source code is as follows:

```
examplestring = " In a galaxy far away"
print(examplestring.lstrip())
examplestring = "In a galaxy far away "
print(examplestring.rstrip())
examplestring = " In a galaxy far away "
print(examplestring.strip())
```

The execution of the above source code has the following output:

```
================ RESTART: /Users/alfre/Desktop/Python/2-5-10.py ================
In a galaxy far away
In a galaxy far away
In a galaxy far away
>>>
```

The eleventh exercise of the phase consists of learning the instructions *max* and *min*, which allows you to know the major and minor alphabetical character of the text string. The exercise executes the instructions with a text string, and the screen shows the major and the minor characters. The source code is as follows.

```
examplestring = "abcdefghijklmnopqrstuvwxyz"
print(max(examplestring))
print(min(examplestring))
```

The execution of the above source code has the following output:

```
================ RESTART: /Users/alfre/Desktop/Python/2-5-11.py ================
z
a
>>>
```

The twelfth exercise of the phase consists of learning the *replace* instruction, which allows you to replace characters in the text string by other characters. The exercise replaces a character of the string. The screen displays the result of the replacement. The source code is as follows:

```
examplestring = "AEIOU"
print(examplestring.replace('A','E'))
```

The execution of the above source code has the following output:

```
================ RESTART: /Users/alfre/Desktop/Python/2-5-12.py ================
EEIOU
>>>
```

In the thirteenth exercise of the phase, we explain the *swapcase* instruction. The instruction allows you to convert letters from upper case to lower case, and vice-versa. The exercise executes the instruction with a text string. The screen displays the result of the operation. The source code is as follows:

```
examplestring = "In a galaxy far away"
print(examplestring.swapcase())
```

The execution of the above source code has the following output:

```
================ RESTART: /Users/alfre/Desktop/Python/2-5-13.py ================
iN A GALAXY FAR AWAY
>>>
```

The fourteenth exercise of the phase consists of learning the *split* instruction, which allows you to convert a text string into a list of elements that are separated by spaces in the original text string. The exercise executes the instruction on a text string. The screen displays the resulting list. The source code is as follows:

```
examplestring = "In a galaxy far away"
print(examplestring.split())
```

The execution of the above source code has the following output:

```
================ RESTART: /Users/alfre/Desktop/Python/2-5-14.py ================
['In', 'a', 'galaxy', 'far', 'away']
>>>
```

The fifteenth exercise of the phase consists of expanding the use of the *split* command, but this time, indicating the character to use to separate the elements of the list. The way of indicating the character to use is by a string parameter with the *split* command. The exercise executes the instruction on a text string. The screen displays the result of the operation. The source code is as follows:

```
examplestring = "31/12/2020"
print(examplestring.split("/"))
```

The execution of the above source code has the following output:

```
================ RESTART: /Users/alfre/Desktop/Python/2-5-15.py ================
['31', '12', '2020']
>>>
```

## NOW YOU CAN...

In this second objective, you have learned the following knowledge:

- Data types in Python.
- Use of integer and real numbers.
- Use of arithmetical operators.

- Use of relational operators.
- Use of logical operators.
- Use of booleans.
- Use of text strings.
- Manipulation of text strings.
- Use of lists, tuples and dictionaries.
- Data conversion.

In this third objective, we explain how to use the instruction that allows controlling the flow of the programs, the bifurcation.

The objective contains three phases. You learn to use simple bifurcations in the first phase. In the second, you learn to use bifurcations with an alternative path. Finally, in the third, you learn to use bifurcations with more than one alternative path.

## THEORETICAL CONCEPTS

In this section, in addition to explaining the theory of bifurcations, we explain what instruction blocks are, how the indentation works in Python and why it is essential and necessary when writing your programs.

## BLOCKS AND INDENTATION

A block is a group of source code statements that contains one or more statements. Blocks have a beginning and an end, and the way to delimit them is specific to each programming language.

Indentation means moving a block of text to the right by inserting spaces or tabs, to separate it from the left margin and to distinguish it more easily within the text. All languages use indentation to increase the readability of the source code. Still, in Python, it is not only an aesthetic practice, since it uses the indentation of the source code to delimit the blocks within the source code. You have to use blocks correctly. Let's see an example with an image:

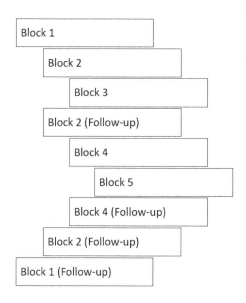

In the image, you can see different blocks of code that in turn, have other blocks within them. A code block can contain more than one code block inside, and they are called internal blocks. Internal blocks are "like" statements inside parent blocks.

## IF / ELIF /ELSE

You have to understand bifurcations in programming as the existence of different possible paths based on a condition or conditions. The instructions that allow you to use bifurcations are *if*, *elif* and *else*. Let's see them in detail:

- **if**: it allows you to generate a code block that executes if the input condition is *true*.
- **elif**: it allows you to generate an alternative path with an input condition.

- **else**: it allows you to generate an alternative path that executes as long as the conditions of the possible paths of the *if* and *elif* instructions have not been satisfied.

Let's see it with an example as complete as possible. Note that this source code is not Python:

*number1 = RandomValue*
*number2 = RandomValue*

*if number1>number2*
    *InstructionBlock1*
*elif number1==number2*
    *InstructionBlock2*
*else*
    *InstructionBlock3*

In the example, we have defined two variables whose values generate randomly. Using these variables, we have generated three possible paths:

- **if number1> number2**: if the first number is higher than the second, the block of instructions called *InstructionBlock1* executes.
- **elif number1 == number2**: if the first number and the second are the same, the block of instructions called *InstructionBlock2* executes.
- **else**: if the first number is less than the second number, the block of instructions called *InstructionBlock3* executes. In this case, it is not necessary to establish a condition. Since when comparing numbers, there are only three possibilities, that the first is less than the second, that both are equal or that the first is greater than the second.

Finally, we indicate that within the blocks of instructions that are within the possible paths, it is possible to include new bifurcations. In this case, we would be talking about nested bifurcations.

## PHASE 1: IF STATEMENT

The first phase of this objective consists of learning how to use the *if* statement. Using this statement, you can create a code block that executes if the input condition specified in the statement is *true*.

The first exercise in the phase consists of evaluating the value of a number entered by the user. If the number is greater than 10, a message displays on the screen.

With the symbol "+" inside *print*, you can join the text string *"You have written the number"* with the number to display the message on the screen. Note that you have to convert the number that you have used to make the comparison into a text string to display it on the screen using the *print* command. For this, you have to use *str(number)*.

The source code is as follows:

```
number = int(input("Enter a number in the range 0-10: "))
if number>10:
    print("The number is higher than 10!")
print("Number entered: " + str(number))
```

The execution of the above source code has the following possible outputs based on the number entered:

The number greater than 10:

```
================= RESTART: /Users/alfre/Desktop/Python/3-1-1.py =================
Enter a number in the range 0-10: 13
The number is higher than 10!
Number entered: 13
>>>
```

The number less than 10 or equal to 10:

```
================ RESTART: /Users/alfre/Desktop/Python/3-1-1.py ===============
Enter a number in the range 0-10: 5
Number entered: 5
>>>
```

## PHASE 2: IF..ELSE STATEMENT

The second phase of this objective consists of learning the *if..else* statement. Using this statement, you can create two different blocks of code. One that executes whenever the input condition is *true* (block within *if*) and another that executes whenever the input condition is *false* (block within *else*).

The first exercise in the phase consists of searching for a specific text within a text string and showing on the screen, whether it exists or not in the text. In this exercise, you learn a new way to search a string of text within another. The source code is as follows:

```
examplestring = "In a galaxy far away..."
if "galaxy" in examplestring:
    print("Found!")
else:
    print("Not found!")
```

The execution of the above source code has the following output:

```
================ RESTART: /Users/alfre/Desktop/Python/3-2-1.py
Found!
>>>
```

Try to write a text that does not appear in the string instead of "galaxy", and you see how the block of *else* instructions executes.

The second exercise in the phase consists of checking the start and end characters of a text string and showing on the screen whether or not they start with these characters. The source code is as follows:

```
examplestring = "In a galaxy far away"
if examplestring.startswith('I'):
    print("Starts with I!")
else:
    print("Doesn't start with I!")
if examplestring.endswith('p'):
    print("Finishes with p!")
else:
    print("Doesn't finish with p!")
```

The execution of the above source code has the following output:

```
================== RESTART: /Users/alfre/Desktop/Python/3-2-2.py =================
Starts with I!
Doesn't finish with p!
>>>
```

Try changing the characters that the *startswith* and *endswith* functions receive as parameters, and you see how different blocks execute in the bifurcations.

## PHASE 3: IF..ELIF..ELSE STATEMENT

The third phase of this objective consists of learning the *if..elif..else* statement. Using this sentence, you can create infinite alternative paths depending on the fulfilment of the entry condition.

The first exercise in the phase consists of the implementation in Python of the example we have used in the theoretical explanation. Still, instead of generating the number randomly, we ask for it to the user. The source code is as follows:

```
number1 = int(input("Enter the first number (integer): "))
number2 = int(input("Enter the second number (integer): "))
if number1>number2:
    print("First number higher than second number")
elif number1==number2:
    print("Number are equals")
else:
    print("First number lower than second number")
```

67

The execution of the above source code has the following possible outputs depending on the entered values:

### The first number higher than the second:

```
================ RESTART: /Users/alfre/Desktop/Python/3-3-1.py ================
Enter the first number (integer): 23
Enter the second number (integer): 12
First number higher than second number
>>>
```

### Both numbers equal:

```
================ RESTART: /Users/alfre/Desktop/Python/3-3-1.py ================
Enter the first number (integer): 7
Enter the second number (integer): 7
Number are equals
>>>
```

### The first number less than the second:

```
================ RESTART: /Users/alfre/Desktop/Python/3-3-1.py ================
Enter the first number (integer): 45
Enter the second number (integer): 89
First number lower than second number
>>>
```

## NOW YOU CAN...

In this third objective, you have learned the following knowledge:

- Use of bifurcations:
    - if
    - if..else
    - if..elif..else
- Start using operating logic in programs.
- Use of *startswith*, *endswith* and *search* methods of strings.

In this fourth objective, you learn to use the programming structures known as loops.

The objective contains three phases. In the first, you learn to use *while* loops, in the second you learn to use *for* loops and in the last, you learn to use *nested loops*.

## THEORETICAL CONCEPTS

In this section, we explain what a loop is and the different types of loops that are available in Python.

### LOOP

Loops consist of the execution repetition of an instruction block; each repetition is called iteration. In programming, there are different types of loops; you use each one depending on the usage context.

In a loop, you have to specify the following:

- Loop start point.
- Loop endpoint.
- The number of iterations.

Each type of loop specifies the previous points differently, but with the same theoretical meaning.

Let's see the different loops that we have available in Python.

## FOR

We recommend using the *for* loop type in contexts in which you know the exact iterations number. It is a loop that executes a set of instructions repeatedly until reaching the maximum number of defined iterations.

In Python, *for* loops runs on iterable elements, such as lists, tuples, text strings, or dictionaries. The number of iterations to run depends on the number of elements the iterable element contains.

For loops have the following syntax:

*for Variable in IterableCollection:*
    *InstructionBlock*

Let's see the elements in detail:

- for: loop start indicator.
- Variable: the variable that stores the element on which *IterableCollection* is iterating.
- in: indicator used to define the iterable element on which the for loop executes.
- IterableCollection: element on which the loop iterates.
- InstructionBlock: the set of instructions that execute in each iteration.

## WHILE

We recommend using the while loop type in contexts in which you do not know the exact iterations number. Still, the iterations execute until the condition that verifies in each iteration is *true*.

The condition used to check if an iteration has to execute must be *true* for it to execute. If the condition is false, the execution of the loop ends. The loop checks the condition at each iteration of the loop. The variables used in the loop condition are called control variables.

While loops have the following syntax:

*while Condition:*
    *InstructionBlock*

Let's see the elements in detail:

- while: loop start indicator.
- Condition: the condition that must fulfil to go ahead with the execution of the instruction block.
- InstructionBlock: the set of instructions that execute in each iteration.

When using while loops, you may run into the following problems:

- Loops that never execute: pay special attention to the initialization of the loop control variables. Make sure that the condition is *true* because if the condition is *false* from the beginning, the loop never executes.
- Infinite loops: pay special attention to modifying the values of the loop control variables within the loop, since, if these values never change, the loop never stops executing.

## PHASE 1: WHILE LOOP

The first phase of this objective consists of learning how to use the *while* loop.

The first exercise of the phase consists of executing a *while* loop where the value of the control variable *i* is displayed. The source code is as follows:

```
i = 0
while i<10:
    print(i,end=" ")
    i = i + 1
```

As you can see in the code, before starting the loop execution, the control variable of the loop initializes with the value 0. Furthermore, within the instructions block, its value is being altered to ensure the loop condition reaches a *false* value, which occurs when the value of the control variable is 10.

The execution of the above source code has the following output:

```
================= RESTART: /Users/alfre/Desktop/Python/4-1-1.py ================
0 1 2 3 4 5 6 7 8 9
>>>
```

The second exercise in the phase consists of executing a *while* loop in which the condition is a boolean. The value changes if the number entered by the user inside the loop is greater than 100. The source code is as follows:

```
notfinish = True
while notfinish:
    value = int(input("Enter a number higher than 100 (integer): "))
    if value>100:
        notfinish = False
print("Program finished")
```

The execution of the above source code has the following output:

```
================= RESTART: /Users/alfre/Desktop/Python/4-1-2.py ================
Enter a number higher than 100 (integer): 68
Enter a number higher than 100 (integer): 91
Enter a number higher than 100 (integer): 103
Program finished
>>>
```

## PHASE 2: FOR LOOP

The second phase of this objective consists of learning how to use the *for* loop.

The first exercise in the phase consists of executing a *for* loop on a list of elements. In each iteration, it shows on the screen the list element on which it is iterating (item). The source code is as follows:

```
itemlist = [1,2,3,4,5,6,7,8,9]
for item in itemlist:
    print(item, end=" ")
```

The execution of the above source code has the following output:

```
================== RESTART: /Users/alfre/Desktop/Python/4-2-1.py ================
1 2 3 4 5 6 7 8 9
>>>
```

The second exercise of the phase is similar to the previous exercise. Still, in this exercise, you go through a list of elements that are text strings. The source code is as follows:

```
itemlist = ["computer", "keyboard", "mouse"]
for item in itemlist:
    print(item, end=" ")
```

The execution of the above source code has the following output:

```
================== RESTART: /Users/alfre/Desktop/Python/4-2-2.py ================
computer keyboard mouse
>>>
```

The third exercise of the phase consists of executing a *for* loop over the elements returned by the *range* instruction. *Range* instruction allows you to obtain a sequential list of integer elements, starting at 0, and with as many elements as indicated in the parameter. In this

73

exercise, the range establishes to return a list from 0 to 9. In each iteration, it shows on the screen the value of the element that is iterating. The source code is as follows:

```
for item in range(10):
    print(item, end=" ")
```

The execution of the above source code has the following output:

```
================= RESTART: /Users/alfre/Desktop/Python/4-2-3.py =================
0 1 2 3 4 5 6 7 8 9
>>>
```

## PHASE 3: NESTED LOOPS

The third phase of this objective consists of learning how to use nested loops, which consists of using loops as part of the instruction blocks of other loops. The loop that is inside another loop is usually called an inner loop. In contrast, the loop that contains an inner loop is called an outer loop. You can have the level of nesting you need, that is, a loop within another loop, which in turn is within another loop that is within another loop, etc.

The first exercise in the phase consists of nesting two *for* loops that go through a list of integer elements generated with the range instruction. It shows on the screen in the inner loop instruction block the elements that both loops are iterating over. The source code is as follows:

```
for item1 in range(3):
    for item2 in range(5):
        print("item1 = " + str(item1) + ", item2 = " + str(item2))
```

The execution flow is like this:

- Iteration of the first loop on the first element of the first list (0).

- o Iteration of all elements of the list of the second loop (0 to 4).
- Iteration of the first loop on the second element of the first list (1).
  - o Iteration of all elements of the list of the second loop (0 to 4).
- Iteration of the first loop on the third element of the first list (2).
  - o Iteration of all elements of the list of the second loop (0 to 4).

The inner loop executes entirely as many times as the number of iterations of the outer loop; in this case, the inner loop has executed a total of three times entirely.

The execution of the above source code has the following output:

```
================= RESTART: /Users/alfre/Desktop/Python/4-3-1.py =================
item1 = 0, item2 = 0
item1 = 0, item2 = 1
item1 = 0, item2 = 2
item1 = 0, item2 = 3
item1 = 0, item2 = 4
item1 = 1, item2 = 0
item1 = 1, item2 = 1
item1 = 1, item2 = 2
item1 = 1, item2 = 3
item1 = 1, item2 = 4
item1 = 2, item2 = 0
item1 = 2, item2 = 1
item1 = 2, item2 = 2
item1 = 2, item2 = 3
item1 = 2, item2 = 4
>>>
```

The second exercise in the phase consists of nesting a *while* loop and a *for* loop. The exercise objective is to perform the same previous exercise loop. The outer loop is a *while* loop instead of a *for* loop. The variable *Item1* contains the iterations number of the *while* loop. It is initialized before the loop and increases its value in each iteration. The source code is as follows:

```
item1 = 0
while item1<3:
    for item2 in range(5):
        print("item1 = " + str(item1) + ", item2 = " + str(item2))
    item1 = item1 + 1
```

The execution of the above source code has the following output:

```
================ RESTART: /Users/alfre/Desktop/Python/4-3-2.py ================
item1 = 0, item2 = 0
item1 = 0, item2 = 1
item1 = 0, item2 = 2
item1 = 0, item2 = 3
item1 = 0, item2 = 4
item1 = 1, item2 = 0
item1 = 1, item2 = 1
item1 = 1, item2 = 2
item1 = 1, item2 = 3
item1 = 1, item2 = 4
item1 = 2, item2 = 0
item1 = 2, item2 = 1
item1 = 2, item2 = 2
item1 = 2, item2 = 3
item1 = 2, item2 = 4
>>>
```

The third exercise in the phase consists of the nesting of two *while* loops. In this exercise, you have to keep in mind that for each iteration of the outer loop, you have to initialize the control variables of the inner loop. The goal of the exercise is to perform the same loop as in the previous two exercises. The outer loop is the same as in exercise two. The variable *Item2* contains the iterations number of the inner loop; it is initialized before the loop declaration and increases its value in each loop iteration. The source code is as follows:

```
item1 = 0
while item1<3:
    item2 = 0
    while item2<5:
        print("item1 = " + str(item1) + ", item2 = " + str(item2))
        item2 = item2 + 1
    item1 = item1 + 1
```

The execution of the above source code has the following output:

```
================= RESTART: /Users/alfre/Desktop/Python/4-3-3.py =================
item1 = 0, item2 = 0
item1 = 0, item2 = 1
item1 = 0, item2 = 2
item1 = 0, item2 = 3
item1 = 0, item2 = 4
item1 = 1, item2 = 0
item1 = 1, item2 = 1
item1 = 1, item2 = 2
item1 = 1, item2 = 3
item1 = 1, item2 = 4
item1 = 2, item2 = 0
item1 = 2, item2 = 1
item1 = 2, item2 = 2
item1 = 2, item2 = 3
item1 = 2, item2 = 4
>>>
```

## NOW YOU CAN...

In this fourth objective, you have learned the following knowledge:

- Use of *for* loops.
- Use of *while* loops.
- Use of nested loops.

It is the time for a small project that incorporates everything you have learned so far.

The first project you do is to develop a small calculator that performs the set of the basic operations. In the project, you use the following acquired knowledge:

- Show information on the screen.
- Read of the information entered by users.
- Bifurcations *if..elif.*
- *While* loop.
- NOT logical operator.
- Mathematical operators (+, -, * and /).
- Relational operator ==.

## SOURCE CODE AND EXECUTION

The source code of the project is as follows:

```
end = False
print ("""************
Calculator
************
Menu
1) Sum
2) Subtraction
3) Multiplication
4) Division
5) Exit""")
while not(end):
    opt = int(input("Option:"))
    if (opt==1):
        sum1 = int(input("Sumand one (integer):"))
        sum2 = int(input("Sumand two (integer):"))
        print ("Sum result:", sum1+sum2)
    elif(opt==2):
```

```
    minuend = int(input("Minuend (integer):"))
    subtrahend = int(input("Subtrahend (integer):"))
    print ("Subtraction result:", minuend-subtrahend)
elif(opt==3):
    multiplying = int(input("Multiplying (integer):"))
    multiplier = int(input("Multiplier (integer):"))
    print ("Multiplication result:", multiplying*multiplier)
elif(opt==4):
    dividend = int(input("Dividend (integer):"))
    divider = int(input("Divider (integer):"))
    print ("Division result:", dividend/divider)
elif(opt==5):
    end = True
```

Let's see it in detail.

The program contains a *while* loop that repeats indefinitely until the end control variable takes the value *true*. Using the logical *not* operation, it makes the condition of the loop *false*.

Before starting the execution of the loop, the end control variable initializes, and the menu of options that the user can choose displays on the screen. Pay attention to the way you can write text on the screen using multiple lines. It uses triple quotation marks at the beginning and end of the text string that you want to display on the screen.

Inside the *while* loop is the reading of the option chosen by the user. The *if..elif* structure takes one path or another depending on the operation selected by the user.

The execution of the above source code has the following output:

```
=============== RESTART: /Users/alfre/Desktop/Python/Project1.py ===============
***********
Calculator
***********
Menu
1) Sum
2) Subtraction
3) Multiplication
4) Division
5) Exit
Option:1
Sumand one (integer):34
Sumand two (integer):54
Sum result: 88
Option:2
Minuend (integer):54
Subtrahend (integer):22
Subtraction result: 32
Option:3
Multiplying (integer):4
Multiplier (integer):99
Multiplication result: 396
Option:4
Dividend (integer):33
Divider (integer):11
Division result: 3.0
Option:5
>>>
```

## NOW YOU CAN...

In this first project, you have learned the following knowledge:

- Display text on screen using multiple lines.

In this fifth objective, you learn how to use functions in the source code that you write.

The objective makes up of two phases. In the first, you learn to use simple functions, and in the second, you learn to use nested functions.

## THEORETICAL CONCEPTS

In this section, we explain what functions are.

### FUNCTIONS

A function is a block of source code that contains a set of instructions, and that you can use from the source code that you write as many times as you need.

The functions have the following capabilities:
- They can receive input data to use during the execution.
- They can return data as a result of the execution.

Both capabilities are optional. So, you can have these types of functions:
- Functions that do not receive data and that do not return anything.
- Functions that receive data and that do not return anything.
- Functions that do not receive data and that return data.
- Functions that receive and return data.

The use of functions is beneficial as it brings the following characteristics to the source code:

- Simplification of the code.
- Better organization of the code.
- Reuse of source code.

In short, a function is an independent source code block, which can receive input data and, as a result of its execution, can return data.

The syntax of functions in Python is as follows:

*def FunctionName (parameters):*
    *InstructionBlock*
    *return ReturnedValue*

Let's see the elements in detail:

- def: function definition indicator.
- FunctionName: name that the function has. We advise you to use descriptive function names that represent what the function does.
- Parameters: the set of input elements that the function has. Parameters are optional, that is, there can be 0 or more. In case of being more than one, the parameters are separated by commas.
- InstructionBlock: block of code that executes the function.
- Return: it returns data to the source code used by the function. It is optional, since returning data is not required in functions.
- ReturnedValue: data that is returned.

So far, we have explained how functions are defined in Python, to use functions in Python from the source code you have to do it as follows:

*Variable = FunctionName (parameters)*

Let's see the elements in detail:

- Variable: it stores the value that the function returns. It is optional; it means that you can omit it if the function returns nothing.
- FunctionName: name of the function that we are going to use.
- Parameters: input parameters that the function has and that are separated by commas if there are more than one. It is optional, so if the function does not receive parameters, it omitted.

## PHASE 1: USING A FUNCTION

The first phase of the objective consists of learning the use of functions, both the definition and the usage.

The first exercise in the phase consists of defining the *SayHello* function and subsequent use (also called invocation) from the program. The *SayHello* function does not receive any input parameters neither returns anything; it only writes on the screen. The source code is as follows:

```
def SayHello():
    print("Hello Time of Software!")
SayHello()
```

The execution of the above source code has the following output:

```
================= RESTART: /Users/alfre/Desktop/Python/5-1-1.py =================
Hello Time of Software!
>>>
```

The second exercise of the phase consists of defining the function *IsHigherThanZero*, which checks if the parameter it receives is greater than zero or not and displays a message on the screen indicating it. The invocation of the function uses the number entered by the user as its parameter. The source code is as follows:

```
def IsHigherThanZero(param):
    if param > 0:
        print(param, "is higher than zero")
    else:
        print(param, "is not higher than zero")

number = int(input("Enter a number (integer):"))
IsHigherThanZero(number)
```

The execution of the above source code has the following outputs depending on the number entered:

The number less than zero or equal to zero:

```
================= RESTART: /Users/alfre/Desktop/Python/5-1-2.py ================
Enter a number (integer):-5
-5 is not higher than zero
>>>
```

The number higher than zero:

```
================= RESTART: /Users/alfre/Desktop/Python/5-1-2.py ================
Enter a number (integer):7
7 is higher than zero
>>>
```

The third exercise in the phase consists of defining the *Sum* function, which performs the sum of the two parameters it receives as input and returns the result of the sum. The invocation of the function uses the two numbers entered by the user as parameters. The result of the sum displays on the screen. The source code is as follows:

```
def Sum(param1, param2):
    return param1 + param2
sumand1 = int(input("Enter the first summand (integer): "))
sumand2 = int(input("Enter the second summand (integer): "))
result = Sum(sumand1,sumand2)
print("The result of the sum is: ", result)
```

The execution of the above source code has the following output:

```
================ RESTART: /Users/alfre/Desktop/Python/5-1-3.py ================
Enter the first summand (integer): 34
Enter the second summand (integer): 23
The result of the sum is:  57
>>>
```

The fourth exercise of the phase consists of the function definition of *SumSubtract*, which performs the addition and subtraction of its parameters and returns both operation results. Pay attention to how more than one element is returned and how you can assign each returned value to a different variable. The invocation of the function uses the two numbers entered by the user as parameters. The result of addition and subtraction display on the screen. The source code is as follows:

```
def SumSubtract(param1, param2):
    return param1 + param2, param1 - param2

number1 = int(input("Enter the first number (integer): "))
number2 = int(input("Enter the second number (integer): "))
sumresult, subtractionresult = SumSubtract(number1,number2)
print("The result of the sum is: ", sumresult)
print("The result of the subtraction is: ", subtractionresult)
```

The execution of the above source code has the following output:

```
================ RESTART: /Users/alfre/Desktop/Python/5-1-4.py ================
Enter the first number (integer): 67
Enter the second number (integer): 34
The result of the sum is:  101
The result of the subtraction is:  33
>>>
```

The fifth exercise of the phase consists of defining the *Sum* function, which adds all the values passed to it as a parameter. Pay attention to how the parameters of the function are defined. This way, you can pass to the function only a parameter, or three parameters, or ten parameters, etc., and the function only has defined one parameter. In these functions, the parameter is a list, so you have to iterate it to

85

be able to process all of them. The result of the *sum* displays on the screen. The source code is as follows:

```
def Sum(*values):
    result = 0
    for item in values:
        result = result + item
    return result

result = Sum(23,56,3,89,78,455)
print("The result of the sum is: ", result)
```

The execution of the above source code has the following output:

```
================ RESTART: /Users/alfre/Desktop/Python/5-1-5.py ================
The result of the sum is:   704
>>>
```

## PHASE 2: NESTED FUNCTIONS

The second phase of the objective consists of learning the use of functions from within functions. This way, you can simplify the code and reuse functions that you have already developed in the new functions that you develop.

The first exercise of the phase is an evolution of the fourth exercise of the first phase of this objective. As you can see, instead of performing the addition and subtraction operations directly in the *SumSubtract* function, we use the *Sum* and *Subtract* functions. The source code is as follows:

```
def SumSubtract(param1, param2):
    return Sum(param1,param2), Subtract(param1,param2)

def Sum(sumand1, sumand2):
    return sumand1 + sumand2

def Subtract(minuend, subtrahend):
    return minuend - subtrahend
```

86

```
number1 = int(input("Enter the first number (integer): "))
number2 = int(input("Enter the second number (integer): "))
sumresult, subtractionresult = SumSubtract(number1,number2)
print("The result of the sum is: ", sumresult)
print("The result of the subtraction is: ", subtractionresult)
```

The execution of the above source code has the following output:

```
================= RESTART: /Users/alfre/Desktop/Python/5-2-1.py =================
Enter the first number (integer): 34
Enter the second number (integer): 22
The result of the sum is:  56
The result of the subtraction is:  12
>>>
```

## NOW YOU CAN...

In this fifth objective, you have learned the following knowledge:

- Creation of functions.
- Use of functions in your source code.
- Nested functions.

Now it is time to do the second project in the book. It is an evolutionary project of project number one in which you developed a calculator.

The project consists of applying the knowledge that you have acquired in the previous objective regarding functions to create a version that is easier to read, orderly and reusable.

## SOURCE CODE AND EXECUTION

The evolutionary project consists of the creation of the following functions:

- Add: it is in charge of carrying out the entire addition process.
- Subtract: it is in charge of the entire subtraction process.
- Multiplication: it is in charge of the entire multiplication process.
- Divide: it is in charge of the entire dividing process.
- Calculator: it is in charge of executing the loop and asking the user for the option to execute.

Once you have the functions created, you have to create the source code to show the options and the invocation statement of the *Calculator* function. The source code is as follows:

```
def Sum():
    sum1 = int(input("Sumand one (integer):"))
    sum2 = int(input("Sumand two (integer):"))
    print ("Sum result:", sum1+sum2)

def Subtraction():
    minuend = int(input("Minuend (integer):"))
```

```python
    subtrahend = int(input("Subtrahend (integer):"))
    print ("Subtraction result:", minuend-subtrahend)

def Multiplication():
    multiplying = int(input("Multiplying (integer):"))
    multiplier = int(input("Multiplier (integer):"))
    print ("Multiplication result:", multiplying*multiplier)

def Division():
    dividend = int(input("Dividend (integer):"))
    divider = int(input("Divider (integer):"))
    print ("Division result:", dividend/divider)

def Calculator():
    end = False
    while not(end):
        opt = int(input("Option:"))
        if (opt==1):
            Sum()
        elif(opt==2):
            Subtraction()
        elif(opt==3):
            Multiplication()
        elif(opt==4):
            Division()
        elif(opt==5):
            end = 1

print ("""************
Calculator
************
Menu
1) Sum
2) Subtraction
3) Multiplication
4) Division
5) Exit""")
Calculator()
```

The execution of the above source code has the following output:

```
=============== RESTART: /Users/alfre/Desktop/Python/Project2.py ===============
************
Calculator
************
Menu
1) Sum
2) Subtraction
3) Multiplication
4) Division
5) Exit
Option:1
Sumand one (integer):54
Sumand two (integer):78
Sum result: 132
Option:2
Minuend (integer):334
Subtrahend (integer):22
Subtraction result: 312
Option:3
Multiplying (integer):67
Multiplier (integer):4
Multiplication result: 268
Option:4
Dividend (integer):783
Divider (integer):3
Division result: 261.0
Option:5
>>>
```

## NOW YOU CAN...

In this second project, you have learned the following knowledge:

- Organize the source code with functions.

In this sixth objective, you learn what object-oriented programming is, and also, you learn how to use it in your programs.

The objective is composed of two phases. In the first phase, you learn to use simple classes so that you can correctly consolidate the new concepts. In the second phase, you learn to use class composition.

## THEORETICAL CONCEPTS

In this section, we are going to explain all the theoretical concepts you need to know about object-oriented programming.

## PARADIGM SHIFT

The world of software development is in constant evolution and change, and back in the 1960s, people began to talk about a new development paradigm, which was object-oriented programming. The objective of object-oriented programming had no other objective than to try to alleviate the existing deficiencies in programming at that time, which were the following:

- **A different abstraction of the world**: programming at that time focused on behaviours usually represented by verbs, while object-oriented programming focused on beings, usually represented by nouns. **It goes from using functions that represent verbs to using classes that represent nouns**.
- **The difficulty of modification and updating**: the programs usually share the data, so any slight modification

of the data could cause indirectly that another program stops working.

- **The difficulty of maintenance**: the bug fixing that existed at the time were quite expensive and challenging to perform.
- **The difficulty of reuse**: functions/routines are usually highly dependent on the context in which they are created, and that makes it difficult to reuse them in new programs.

Object-oriented programming appeared to contribute to the following:

- A new abstraction of the world centring it on **beings** and not on verbs through new concepts such as **class** and **object** that we see in the next section.
- Data access control through **encapsulation** of data in classes.
- A new set of features for classes that simplify the development. Such as **inheritance** and **composition**.

## CLASS AND OBJECT CONCEPTS

Before we begin, we are going to do a simile of object-oriented programming with the real world. Look around you. What do you see? The answer is objects. We surrounded by objects, such as cars, lamps, telephones, tablets, etc. The new paradigm of object-oriented programming bases on a real-world abstraction. It allows us to develop programs closer to how we see the world, thinking in objects in front of us and actions that we can perform with them.

A **class** is a type of data whose variables are called **objects** or **instances**. That is, the class is the definition of the concept of the real world, and the objects or instances are the "object" of the real world. Think for a second about a car, before manufactured it, a car has to be defined; it needs to have a template that specifies its components and what it can do. **That template is what is known as Class. Once the car builds, it is an object or instance of the Car class.**

Classes can contain two elements:

- **Attributes**: information that the class stores.
- **Methods**: operations that the class performs.

Now think about the car from before, the car class could have attributes such as the number of gears, the number of seats, engine size, etc. It could perform operations such as upshifting, downshifting, accelerating, braking, turning on the indicator, etc. An object is a specific model car.

A class in Python defines as follows:

*class ClassName:*
 *def __init__ (self, parameter1, parameter2):*
  *InstructionBlockConstructor*
 *def Method1(self):*
  *InstructionBlock1*
 *def Method2(self, methodparameter1):*
  *InstructionBlock2*

Let's see each component in isolation:
- class: identifier to define a class.
- className: name that the class has.
- def: identifier to define methods of the class.
- __init__: an identifier that defines the constructor of the class.

- self.Attributes: attributes that the class has. It is necessary to specify them with *"self."* before the name of the attribute.
- Parameters: list of parameters that the constructor and methods receive.
- Methods: methods that the class has.
- InstructionBlock: a set of instructions that each method or constructor have.

During the phases, we go deep in the class structure.

## COMPOSITION

The composition consists of the creation of new classes from other existing classes that act as composer elements of the new one. It means that the existing classes are attributes of the new class. The composition allows you to reuse source code.

When we talk about composition you have to think that between the two classes there is a relationship of the type **"has a"**.

## PHASE 1: SIMPLE CLASS

The first phase of the objective consists of learning and using the classes and objects.

In all the classes you create, it is always necessary to create a method called *"__init__"*. It is what is known as the class constructor or initializer. It is possible to include parameters; the way to specify them is the same as in functions. The *"__init__"* method is the first thing that executes when you create an object of a class.

The first exercise of the phase consists of creating a class that represents a point, with its X coordinate and its Y coordinate. Also, the class has a method to display the information that both points have. The exercise consists of creating an object or instance (*p1*) of the class, establishing the coordinates and using the method to display the coordinate information. The source code is as follows:

```
class Point:
    def __init__ (self, x, y):
        self.X = x
        self.Y = y
    def ShowPoint(self):
        print("The point is (",self.X,",",self.Y,")")

p1 = Point(4,6)
p1.ShowPoint()
```

The statement "*p1 = Point (4,6)*" is the statement in which an object of class *Point* is created and stored in the variable *p1*. Pay close attention to how objects are created; you use it in all the exercises. The type of data that variable *p1* contains is *Point*.

The execution of the above source code has the following output:

```
================ RESTART: /Users/alfre/Desktop/Python/6-1-1.py ================
The point is ( 4 , 6 )
>>>
```

The second exercise of the phase consists of doing the same as in the previous exercise but this time creating four objects of the class Point (*p1, p2, p3 and p4*). Each object has its coordinate values. After creating the four objects, the information stored by each of them displays on the screen. The source code is as follows:

```
class Point:
    def __init__ (self, x, y):
        self.X = x
        self.Y = y
    def ShowPoint(self):
        print("Point values (",self.X,",",self.Y,")")
```

```
p1 = Point(4,6)
p2 = Point(-5,9)
p3 = Point(3,-7)
p4 = Point(0,4)
p1.ShowPoint()
p2.ShowPoint()
p3.ShowPoint()
p4.ShowPoint()
```

The execution of the above source code has the following output:

```
================ RESTART: /Users/alfre/Desktop/Python/6-1-2.py ================
Point values ( 4 , 6 )
Point values ( -5 , 9 )
Point values ( 3 , -7 )
Point values ( 0 , 4 )
>>>
```

The third exercise of the phase has the learning objective to modify the information that an object of a class has stored. To do this, we create an object of class *Point*, and we modify the information of one of its coordinates. The way to access the attributes is *Object.AttributeName*. The information about the object before and after the modification displays on the screen. The source code is as follows:

```
class Point:
    def __init__ (self, x, y):
        self.X = x
        self.Y = y
    def ShowPoint(self):
        print("Point value (",self.X,",",self.Y,")")

p1 = Point(4,6)
p1.ShowPoint()
p1.X = 7
p1.ShowPoint()
```

The execution of the above source code has the following output:

```
================ RESTART: /Users/alfre/Desktop/Python/6-1-3.py ================
Point value ( 4 , 6 )
Point value ( 7 , 6 )
>>>
```

The fourth exercise of the phase consists of learning that assigning objects, the values that the object has in its attributes are assigned to the target object. In the exercise, two objects of the *Point* class are created and displayed on the screen, and one of them assigned to the other. The assignment target object displays on the screen to check that the information has modified. The source code is as follows:

```
class Point:
    def __init__(self, x, y):
        self.X = x
        self.Y = y
    def ShowPoint(self):
        print("Point values (",self.X,",",self.Y,")")

p1 = Point(4,6)
p1.ShowPoint()
p2 = Point(3,8)
p2.ShowPoint()
p1 = p2
p1.ShowPoint()
```

The execution of the above source code has the following output:

```
================ RESTART: /Users/alfre/Desktop/Python/6-1-4.py ================
Point values ( 4 , 6 )
Point values ( 3 , 8 )
Point values ( 3 , 8 )
>>>
```

As you can see, the information of the object *p1* updated with the information of the object *p2*.

## PHASE 2: COMPOSITION

The second phase of the objective consists of learning and using the composition of classes.

The first exercise of the phase consists of learning how to use classes as attributes of other classes. Having the class that we have been using in the last phase, we define a new class called *Triangle*, which contains three *Point* attributes. As we have explained, you do not have to specify the data type of the attributes, so creating three attributes is enough. Besides, you have to create a method in the *Triangle* class that shows the information of each of the attributes using the method that the *Point* class has for it. The exercise consists of creating three objects of *Point* class and one object of *Triangle* class that receives the three objects of the *Point* class as parameters. Finally, the information of the *Triangle* class is displayed using the *ShowVertices* method that displays the information of the three attributes using the *ShowPoint* method of the *Point* class. The source code is as follows:

```
class Point:
    def __init__ (self, x, y):
        self.X = x
        self.Y = y
    def ShowPoint(self):
        print("Point value (",self.X,",",self.Y,")")

class Triangle:
    def __init__ (self, v1,v2,v3):
        self.V1 = v1
        self.V2 = v2
        self.V3 = v3
    def ShowVertices(self):
        self.V1.ShowPoint()
        self.V2.ShowPoint()
        self.V3.ShowPoint()

v1 = Point(3,4)
v2 = Point(6,8)
v3 = Point(9,2)
triangle = Triangle(v1,v2,v3)
triangle.ShowVertices()
```

The execution of the above source code has the following output:

```
================ RESTART: /Users/alfre/Desktop/Python/6-2-1.py ================
Point value ( 3 , 4 )
Point value ( 6 , 8 )
Point value ( 9 , 2 )
>>>
```

NOW YOU CAN...

In this sixth objective, you have learned the following knowledge:

- Creation of classes.
- Difference between class and object or instance.
- Use of classes in your programs.
- Access to class attributes.
- Access to class methods.
- Class composition.

Now is the time to do the third project of the book, a project in which you are going to consolidate the knowledge acquired in the previous objective about object-oriented programming.

In the project, you use all the knowledge of the last objectives to create a simple application that allows you to simulate the management of a library. In the project, you use the following knowledge acquired since you started the book:

- Show information on the screen.
- Read of the information entered by the user.
- Use of primary data: numbers, text strings and lists.
- *While* loop.
- *For* loop.
- Bifurcations *if..elif*.
- Creation and use of functions.
- Object-oriented programming.
- Class composition.

## SOURCE CODE AND EXECUTION

The project, although it is much more extensive than everything you have done so far, is straightforward. Next, we are going to explain everything that you are going to develop.

The library that you are going to develop contains the following three classes:

- **Author**: the class that contains all the information about the person who wrote the book.

- **Book**: the class that contains all the information about the book.
- **Library**: the class that contains all books that make up the library.

Let's see the classes in detail.

## Author Class

The **Author** class is composed of the following attributes:

- Name: the name of the writer.
- LastName: the last name of the writer.

The Author class is composed of the following methods:

- ShowAuthor: it displays the first name and the last name attributes on the screen.

## Book Class

The **Book** class is composed of the following attributes:

- Title: name of the book.
- ISBN: book identifier.
- Author: attribute of type Author.

The **Book** class is composed of the following methods:

- AddAuthor: it stores the author information in the Author attribute.
- ShowBook: it displays the book information on the screen.
- GetTitle: it returns the title of the book.

## Library class

The **Library** class is composed of the following attributes:

- BookList: list type attribute that contains all books that make up the library.

The **Library** class is composed of the following methods:

- NumberOfBooks: it returns the number of books that make up the library.
- AddBook: it stores the book passed by the parameter in the list of books it has as an attribute.
- DeleteBook: it deletes a book from the library based on its title.
- ShowLibrary: it displays all the books that make up the library on the screen.

## Functions

Now let's see the different functions that the project contains:

- **ShowMenu**: a function that shows the options menu to the users so that they can choose what they want to do with the program.
- **AddBookToLibrary**: a function that carries out the flow of registering a new book in the library. It requests the user all the information necessary for a book.
- **ShowLibrary**: function that using the *ShowLibrary* method of the Library class shows the information about all the books that make up the library.
- **DeleteBookFronLibrary**: a function that performs the flow of removing (deleting) a book from the library.

- **NumberOfBooks**: a function that shows on the screen the number of books that make up the library.

## Program

The program consists of a loop that displays the menu. Depending on the option chosen, it executes one operation or another. The available options are as follows:

1. Add a book to the library.
2. Show the library.
3. Delete a book from the library.
4. Show the number of books that make up the library.
5. Exit.

The source code would be the following:

```
class Author:
    def __init__ (self, name, lastname):
        self.Name = name
        self.LastName = lastname
    def ShowAuthor(self):
        print("Author: ",self.Name," ",self.LastName)

class Book:
    def __init__ (self, title, isbn):
        self.Title = title
        self.ISBN = isbn
    def AddAuthor(self, author):
        self.Author = author
    def ShowBook(self):
        print("------ Book ------")
        print("Title: ",self.Title)
        print("ISBN: ", self.ISBN)
        self.Author.ShowAuthor()
        print("------------------")
    def GetTitle(self):
        return self.Title

class Library:
    def __init__(self):
```

103

```python
    self.BookList = []
    def NumberOfBooks(self):
        return len(self.BookList)
    def AddBook(self,book):
        self.BookList = self.BookList + [book]
    def ShowLibrary(self):
        print("####################################")
        for item in self.BookList:
            item.ShowBook()
        print("####################################")
    def DeleteBook(self, title):
        found = False
        positiontodelete = -1
        for item in self.BookList:
            positiontodelete += 1
            if item.GetTitle() == title:
                found = True
                break
        if found:
            del self.BookList[positiontodelete]
            print("Book deleted correctly!")
        else:
            print("Book not found!")

def ShowMenu():
    print ("""Menu
1) Add book to library
2) Show library
3) Delete book from library
4) Number of books?
5) Exit""")

def AddBookToLibrary(library):
    title = input("Enter the title of the book: ")
    isbn = input("Enter the ISBN of the book: ")
    authorname = input("Enter the name of the author: ")
    authorlastname = input("Enter the last name of the author: ")
    author = Author(authorname,authorlastname)
    book = Book(title, isbn)
    book.AddAuthor(author)
    library.AddBook(book)
    return library

def ShowLibrary(library):
    library.ShowLibrary()

def DeleteBookFronLibrary(library):
```

```
title = input("Enter the title of the book to delete: ")
library.DeleteBook(title)

def NumberOfBooks(library):
    print("The number of books of the library is: ",library.NumberOfBooks())

end = False
library = Library()

while not end:
    ShowMenu()
    option = int(input("Select an option:"))
    if(option == 1):
        library = AddBookToLibrary(library)
    elif(option == 2):
        ShowLibrary(library)
    elif(option == 3):
        DeleteBookFronLibrary(library)
    elif(option == 4):
        NumberOfBooks(library)
    elif(option == 5):
        end = True

print("Goodbye!")
```

Let's see the output of the execution. In the following image, you can see the addition of two books to the library (*Option 1*) and the display of the number of books that make up the library (*Option 4*).

```
=============== RESTART: /Users/alfre/Desktop/Python/Project3.py ===============
Menu
1) Add book to library
2) Show library
3) Delete book from library
4) Number of books?
5) Exit
Select an option:1
Enter the title of the book: The Lord of the Rings
Enter the ISBN of the book: 978-0261103207
Enter the name of the author: J.R.R.
Enter the last name of the author: Tolkien
Menu
1) Add book to library
2) Show library
3) Delete book from library
4) Number of books?
5) Exit
Select an option:1
Enter the title of the book: Game of Thrones
Enter the ISBN of the book: 978-1613832776
Enter the name of the author: George R.R.
Enter the last name of the author: Martin
Menu
1) Add book to library
2) Show library
3) Delete book from library
4) Number of books?
5) Exit
Select an option:4
The number of books of the library is:  2
```

In the following image, you can see how the application looks when you show all the books that make up the library (*Option 2*):

```
Menu
1) Add book to library
2) Show library
3) Delete book from library
4) Number of books?
5) Exit
Select an option:2
#####################################
------- Book ------
Title:  The Lord of the Rings
ISBN:   978-0261103207
Author:  J.R.R.   Tolkien
--------------------
------- Book ------
Title:  Game of Thrones
ISBN:   978-1613832776
Author:  George R.R.   Martin
--------------------
#####################################
```

Finally, in the following image, you can see the process of deleting books from the library (*Option 3*). Also, you can see the subsequent use of showing the number of books that make up the library (*Option 2*) to confirm that the book has deleted. The last option on the menu is to exit (*Option 5*), that ends the program execution.

```
Menu
1) Add book to library
2) Show library
3) Delete book from library
4) Number of books?
5) Exit
Select an option:3
Enter the title of the book to delete: The Lord of the Rings
Book deleted correctly!
Menu
1) Add book to library
2) Show library
3) Delete book from library
4) Number of books?
5) Exit
Select an option:2
#######################################
------ Book ------
Title:  Game of Thrones
ISBN:  978-1613832776
Author:  George R.R.  Martin
--------------------
#######################################
```

## NOW YOU CAN...

In this third project, you have learned the following knowledge:

- Creation of a full program from scratch using object-oriented programming.
- Structure of the source code from the beginning of the development.

In this seventh objective, you learn new concepts related to object-oriented programming that allow you to develop more efficiently and in less time.

The objective contains three phases. The first phase is to learn the concept of data encapsulation, the second is to learn the concept of inheritance, and the third is to learn the concept of multiple inheritances.

## THEORETICAL CONCEPTS

In this section, we are going to explain all concepts that you are going to use in this objective.

### ENCAPSULATION

Data encapsulation is the cornerstone of object-oriented programming, which is to protect data (attributes) from uncontrolled access or use. It means that using encapsulation is the class who controls the access to its elements.

The data (attributes) that make up a class can be of two types:

- **Public**: the data is accessible without control.
- **Private**: the data is accessible in a controlled way.

To encapsulate the attributes, what you have to do is **to define the attributes as private and generate a method in the class to access them**. In this way, the class is the only one that accesses the attributes directly, and all external accesses are through the methods defined for this purpose.

**It is also possible to use encapsulation with the methods, not only with the attributes. External elements of the object cannot use those methods that we indicate as private.**

The encapsulation in Python defines as follows:

*class ClassName:*
   *def __init__ (self, parameter1):*
      *self.__PrivateAttribute1*
   *def GetPrivateAttribute1(self):*
      *InstructionBlock1*
   *def SetPrivateAttribute1(self, methodparameter1):*
      *InstructionBlock2*
   *def __PrivateMethod(self):*
      *InstructionBlock3*

Let's see each component:
- class: identifier to define a class.
- className: name that the class has.
- def: identifier to define methods of the class.
- __init__: an identifier that defines the constructor of the class.
- self.__PrivateAttributes: the way of defining private attributes is using "__" (double underscore) before the name of the attribute.
- Parameters: list of parameters that the constructor and methods receive.
- GetPrivateAttribute: it defines a method that returns the information stored in the private attribute.
- SetPrivateAttribute: it defines a method that writes the information received as a parameter in the private attribute.

- InstructionBlock: a set of instructions that each method or constructor has.
- __PrivateMethod: the way of defining private methods is using "__" (double underscore) before the name of the method.

---

## INHERITANCE

Inheritance consists of defining a class using an existing class as a base. The new class is called **derived** (or child) class, and the one from which it inherits is called the **base** (or parent) class. The newly derived class has all the characteristics of the base class and extends its concept; that is, it has all the attributes and methods of the base class. Therefore, the inheritance allows you to reuse source code.

When we talk about inheritance you have to think that between the two classes there is a relationship of the type **"is a"**.

In Python, you define inheritance as follows:

*class BaseClass:*
*    Attributes and methods*
*class **DerivedClass(BaseClass)**:*
*    Attributes and methods*

To use the inheritance, you have to use the base class name inside brackets after the definition of the derived class. That is what you see in bold in the previous example.

## PHASE 1: ENCAPSULATION

The first phase of the objective consists of learning and using the attributes and methods encapsulation.

The first exercise of the phase consists of creating two classes that contain the same information. They differ in that one has its attributes declared as public (*Public Point*), the other has them as private (*Private Point*). It is necessary, for private attributes, that you include the **methods to read** (normally identified by the word *Get* with the name of the attribute as the name of the method). Also, it is necessary to include **methods for writing** (normally identified by the word *Set* with the name of the attribute as the name of the method). The exercise consists in that you see the differences of definition, use and access to the public and private attributes. The private attribute definition does by including the characters *"__"* between the word *"self."* and the attribute name. The source code is as follows:

```
class PublicPoint:
    def __init__ (self, x, y):
        self.X = x
        self.Y = y

class PrivatePoint:
    def __init__ (self, x, y):
        self.__X = x
        self.__Y = y
    def GetX(self):
        return self.__X
    def GetY(self):
        return self.__Y
    def SetX(self, x):
        self.__X = x
    def SetY(self, y):
        self.__Y = y

public = PublicPoint(4,6)
private = PrivatePoint(7,3)
print("Public point values:", public.X,",",public.Y)
print("Private point values:", private.GetX(),",",private.GetY())
public.X = 2
private.SetX(9)
print("Public point values:", public.X,",",public.Y)
print("Private point values:", private.GetX(),",",private.GetY())
```

The execution of the above source code has the following output:

```
================= RESTART: /Users/alfre/Desktop/Python/7-1-1.py ================
Public point values: 4 , 6
Private point values: 7 , 3
Public point values: 2 , 6
Private point values: 9 , 3
>>>
```

The second exercise of the phase consists of learning the encapsulation of the methods of a class. You can define private methods by adding the characters "__" at the beginning of the method name. In the exercise, you are going to define two private methods and a public one through which you use the two private ones. The source code is as follows:

```
class MathOperations:
    def __init__ (self, v1, v2):
        self.__V1 = v1
        self.__V2 = v2
    def __Sum(self):
        return self.__V1 + self.__V2
    def __Subtract(self):
        return self.__V1 - self.__V2
    def Run(self):
        print("The result of the sum is: ",self.__Sum())
        print("The result of the subtraction is: ",self.__Subtract())

operations = MathOperations(7,3)
operations.Run()
```

The execution of the above source code has the following output:

```
================= RESTART: /Users/alfre/Desktop/Python/7-1-2.py ================
The result of the sum is:  10
The result of the subtraction is:  4
>>>
```

The third exercise in the phase consists of checking the error that appears when trying to access a private method. The exercise is the same as in the previous exercise, but invoking one of the private operations of the class. The source code is as follows:

112

```
class MathOperations:
    def __init__ (self, v1, v2):
        self.__V1 = v1
        self.__V2 = v2
    def __Sum(self):
        return self.__V1 + self.__V2
    def __Subtract(self):
        return self.__V1 - self.__V2
    def Run(self):
        print("The result of the sum is: ",self.__Sum())
        print("The result of the subtraction is: ",self.__Subtract())

operations = MathOperations(7,3)
operations.Run()
print("El resultado de la suma es: ",operations.__Sum())
```

The execution of the above source code has the following output:

```
================= RESTART: /Users/alfre/Desktop/Python/7-1-3.py =================
The result of the sum is:  10
The result of the subtraction is:   4
Traceback (most recent call last):
  File "/Users/alfre/Desktop/Python/7-1-3.py", line 15, in <module>
    print("El resultado de la suma es: ",operations.__Sum())
AttributeError: 'MathOperations' object has no attribute '__Sum'
>>>
```

## PHASE 2: INHERITANCE

The second phase of the objective consists of the learning and use of inheritance in object-oriented programming.

The first exercise of the phase consists of the use of a class that is inherited by another. The class that is inherited is a class that we call *Appliance*. It contains a series of attributes and methods that can be inherited by other more specific appliances, such as the washing machine (*Washer class*). To perform the inheritance operation in Python, you only have to add the class you want to inherit from in parentheses in the class header definition. You can check it in the *Washer* class definition in the exercise. The *Washer* class has the attributes and methods of the *Appliance* class available. The

113

exercise consists of creating a *Washer* object and using the methods of both classes (*Washer* and *Appliance*) fill in all the information and display it on the screen. The source code is as follows:

```python
class Appliance:
    def __init__(self):
        self.__IsOn = False
        self.__Voltage = 0
    def TurnOn(self):
        self.__IsOn = True
    def TurnOff(self):
        self.__IsOn = False
    def IsOn(self):
        return self.__IsOn
    def SetVoltage(self, voltage):
        self.__Voltage = voltage
    def GetVoltage(self):
        return self.__Voltage

class Washer(Appliance):
    def __init__(self):
        self.__RPM = 0
        self.__Kilograms = 0
    def SetRPM(self, rpm):
        self.__RPM = rpm
    def SetKilograms(self, kilograms):
        self.__Kilograms = kilograms
    def ShowWasher(self):
        print("#########")
        print("Washer:")
        print("\tRPM:",self.__RPM)
        print("\tKilograms:",self.__Kilograms)
        print("\tVoltage:",self.GetVoltage())
        if self.IsOn():
            print("\tWasher turned on!")
        else:
            print("\tWasher turned off!")
        print("#########")

washer = Washer()
washer.SetRPM(1200)
washer.SetKilograms(7)
washer.SetVoltage(220)
washer.TurnOn()
washer.ShowWasher()
```

The execution of the above source code has the following output:

```
================ RESTART: /Users/alfre/Desktop/Python/7-2-1.py ================
#########
Washer:
     RPM: 1200
     Kilograms: 7
     Voltage: 220
     Washer turned on!
#########
>>>
```

The second exercise in the phase consists of extending the first exercise by creating a new class that also inherits from the *Appliance* class. In this exercise, you create the *Microwave* class, which is a completely different class from *Washer* class but inheriting both from the *Appliance* class. The exercise consists of creating an object of both classes, filling in their information to display them on the screen. The source code is as follows:

```
class Appliance:
    def __init__ (self):
        self.__IsOn = False
        self.__Voltage = 0
    def TurnOn(self):
        self.__IsOn = True
    def TurnOff(self):
        self.__IsOn = False
    def IsOn(self):
        return self.__IsOn
    def SetVoltage(self, voltage):
        self.__Voltage = voltage
    def GetVoltage(self):
        return self.__Voltage

class Washer(Appliance):
    def __init__ (self):
        self.__RPM = 0
        self.__Kilograms = 0
    def SetRPM(self, rpm):
        self.__RPM = rpm
    def SetKilograms(self, kilograms):
        self.__Kilograms = kilograms
    def ShowWasher(self):
        print("#########")
```

115

```python
        print("Washer:")
        print("\tRPM:",self.__RPM)
        print("\tKilograms:",self.__Kilograms)
        print("\tVoltage:",self.GetVoltage())
        if self.IsOn():
            print("\tWasher turned on!")
        else:
            print("\tWasher turned off!")
        print("#########")

class Microwave(Appliance):
    def __init__(self):
        self.__MaximumPower = 0
        self.__Grill = False
    def SetMaximumPower(self, power):
        self.__MaximumPower = power
    def SetGrill(self, grill):
        self.__Grill = grill
    def ShowMicrowave(self):
        print("#########")
        print("Microwave:")
        print("\tMaximum power:",self.__MaximumPower)
        if self.__Grill == True:
            print("\tGrill: Yes")
        else:
            print("\rGrill: No")
        print("\tVoltage:",self.GetVoltage())
        if self.IsOn():
            print("\tMicrowave turned on!")
        else:
            print("\tMicrowave turned off!")
        print("#########")

washer = Washer()
washer.SetRPM(1200)
washer.SetKilograms(7)
washer.SetVoltage(220)
washer.TurnOn()
microwave = Microwave()
microwave.SetMaximumPower(800)
microwave.SetGrill(True)
microwave.SetVoltage(220)
microwave.TurnOff()
washer.ShowWasher()
microwave.ShowMicrowave()
```

The execution of the above source code has the following output:

## PHASE 3: MULTIPLE INHERITANCES

The third phase of the objective consists of the learning and use of multiple inheritances in object-oriented programming. Through multiple inheritances, you can have an object that inherits from more than one class.

The first exercise of the phase consists of creating three different classes in which one of them inherits from the other two. Multiple inheritances is implemented in the same way as single inheritance, but by adding more comma-separated classes to the header of the inheriting class definition. The exercise consists of filling the object information of the class that inherits from the other two and displaying its information on the screen. The source code is as follows:

```
class Hotel:
    def __init__(self):
        self.__NumberOfRooms = 0
        self.__NumberOfStars = 0
    def SetNumberOfRooms(self, rooms):
        self.__NumberOfRooms = rooms
    def SetNumberOfStars(self, stars):
        self.__NumberOfStars = stars
    def ShowHotel(self):
        print("---------")
        print("Hotel:")
        print("\tNumber of stars:", self.__NumberOfStars)
```

117

```python
        print("\tNumber of rooms:", self.__NumberOfRooms)
        print("---------")
class Restaurant:
    def __init__ (self):
        self.__MichelinStars = 0
        self.__OpenTime = 0
    def SetMichelinStars(self, stars):
        self.__MichelinStars = stars
    def SetOpenTime(self, time):
        self.__OpenTime = time
    def ShowRestaurant(self):
        print("---------")
        print("Restaurant:")
        print("\tNumber of Michelin Stars:",self.__MichelinStars)
        print("\tOpen time:",self.__OpenTime)
        print("---------")
class Business(Hotel, Restaurant):
    def __init__(self):
        self.__Name = ""
        self.__Address = ""
        self.__Phone = 0
    def SetName(self, name):
        self.__Name = name
    def SetAddress(self, address):
        self.__Address = address
    def SetPhone(self, phone):
        self.__Phone = phone
    def ShowBusiness(self):
        print("#########")
        print("Business:")
        print("\tName:", self.__Name)
        print("\tAddress:", self.__Address)
        print("\tPhone:", self.__Phone)
        self.ShowHotel()
        self.ShowRestaurant()
        print("#########")
business = Business()
business.SetNumberOfStars(4)
business.SetNumberOfRooms(255)
business.SetMichelinStars(3)
business.SetOpenTime(8)
business.SetName("Time of Software")
business.SetAddress("Calle Falsa 123")
business.SetPhone("0034914567890")
business.ShowBusiness()
```

The execution of the above source code has the following output:

```
================= RESTART: /Users/alfre/Desktop/Python/7-3-1.py =================
#########
Business:
         Name: Time of Software
         Address: Calle Falsa 123
         Phone: 0034914567890
----------
Hotel:
         Number of stars: 4
         Number of rooms: 255
----------
----------
Restaurant:
         Number of Michelin Stars: 3
         Open time: 8
----------
#########
>>>
```

## NOW YOU CAN...

In this seventh objective, you have learned the following knowledge:

- Attributes and methods encapsulation.
- Use of multiple and simple inheritances of classes.

In this eighth objective, you learn to handle the reading and writing of text files. Managing text files is very important since they allow you to read and save information that you use in your programs in files on your computer.

The objective is composed of two phases. In the first phase, you learn to read information stored in text files, and in the second phase, you learn to write information in text files.

## THEORETICAL CONCEPTS

In this section, we are going to explain the theoretical concepts you need to know to work with files in Python.

### FILE MANAGEMENT

Python provides a set of instructions and functions that allows you to perform all allowed operations with files.

Reading and writing text files in Python is done with the **_open_** function, which returns an object that allows you to perform these operations with the file. It is effortless to work with text files in Python.

The open function has two input parameters:

- **Path of the file**: it indicates where the file stores physically.
- **File opening mode**: the way of using the file.

Let's see the different opening modes available:

- **r**: it opens the file for reading. It is the default opening mode if one is not specified.
- **w**: it opens the file for writing by truncating it, that is, deleting all the content it has to start writing again from scratch.
- **x**: it creates a file for writing. In case it already exists, it returns an error.
- **a**: it opens the file for writing by placing the write cursor at the end of the file.
- **b**: it opens the file in binary mode. A binary file is a type of file with information represented in bytes, for example, photographs, executable files, Microsoft Word files, etc.
- **t**: it opens the file in text file mode. It is the default opening mode in case it is not specified to be binary or text.
- **+**: it opens the file for reading and writing.

Once you have finished working with the text file, you need to close the file. For this, you have the *close* function, which allows you to finish working with the file that you previously opened.

In the phases, we explain the different commands that you can use to read and write the files.

## PHASE 1: READING TEXT FILES

The first phase of the objective consists of learning and using all the necessary commands to read text files.

In all the exercises in the phase, you use a text file with content, so you must create a file and write something inside it. The file path can be whatever you prefer. In the exercise, we assumed the file is called "test.txt" and located in the program directory. In the case of you created it in another folder or with another name, you have to modify the parameter file path of the *open* function.

The file "test.txt" that we have used contains the following information:

*Time of Software*
*http://www.timeofsoftware.com*
*Learn Python in a weekend*
*Python is cool*

The first exercise of the phase consists of reading a text file and displaying its content on the screen. The *read* command does the reading, which reads all the file content and stores it as a text string in a variable. The source code is as follows:

```
f = open("test.txt","r")
text = f.read()
print(text)
f.close()
```

The execution of the above source code has the following output:

```
================== RESTART: /Users/alfre/Desktop/Python/8-1-1.py ================
Time of Software
http://www.timeofsoftware.com
Learn Python in a weekend
Python is cool
>>>
```

The second exercise in the phase consists of reading a text file using a *for* loop. Each iteration of the loop reads one line from the file. The exercise reads the text file line by line and displays the lines on the screen. The source code is as follows:

```
for line in open("test.txt","r"):
    print(line)
```

The execution of the above source code has the following output:

```
================ RESTART: /Users/alfre/Desktop/Python/8-1-2.py ================
Time of Software

http://www.timeofsoftware.com

Learn Python in a weekend

Python is cool
>>>
```

The third exercise in the phase consists of reading line by line the text file using the *readline* command. The command returns the content of a single line, leaving the reading cursor on the next line for the next reading. The exercise displays on the screen all the lines. In the exercise we have only included the reading of the first four lines, in case your file has more lines you must include the sentence "*print (f.readline ())*" as many times as the number of lines in your file. The source code is as follows:

```
f = open("test.txt","r")
print(f.readline())
print(f.readline())
print(f.readline())
print(f.readline())
f.close()
```

The execution of the above source code has the following output:

```
================ RESTART: /Users/alfre/Desktop/Python/8-1-3.py ================
Time of Software

http://www.timeofsoftware.com

Learn Python in a weekend

Python is cool
>>>
```

The fourth exercise of the phase consists of reading all lines of the text file with the *readlines* command. The command returns all the file content in an element list where each element is a line of the file. The exercise displays all the lines on the screen. In the exercise, we have only shown the reading of the first four lines. In the case of your file has more lines you must include the statement "*print (lines*

*[X])*", as many times as the number of lines in your file. Also, indicating in the *X* the number of the line you want to display. The source code is as follows:

```
f = open("test.txt","r")
lines = f.readlines()
f.close()
print(lines[0])
print(lines[1])
print(lines[2])
print(lines[3])
```

The execution of the above source code has the following output:

```
================= RESTART: /Users/alfre/Desktop/Python/8-1-4.py =================
Time of Software

http://www.timeofsoftware.com

Learn Python in a weekend

Python is cool
>>>
```

The fifth exercise of the phase consists of doing the same thing you did in the exercise number four, but in a different way. Once the file opens, using the *list* instruction, you obtain a list where each element is a line of the text file. Later, using a *for* loop, the elements of the list are displayed. The source code is as follows:

```
f = open("test.txt","r")
lines = list(f)
f.close()
for item in lines:
    print(item)
```

The execution of the above source code has the following output:

```
================= RESTART: /Users/alfre/Desktop/Python/8-1-5.py =================
Time of Software

http://www.timeofsoftware.com

Learn Python in a weekend

Python is cool
```

## PHASE 2: WRITING TO TEXT FILES

The second phase of the objective consists of learning and using all the necessary commands to write to text files.

The first exercise of the phase consists of learning how to open files in "**a**" mode, that is, open for writing at the end of the file. In the exercise, a new line will be added to an existing file (the one you used in phase 1 of the objective). To check that it is added, the text file is shown before and after the insertion of the new line. The source code is as follows:

```
print("### Initial file ###")
fread = open("test.txt","r")
text = fread.read()
fread.close()
print(text)
print("### Writting lines... ###\n")
fwrite = open("test.txt","a")
fwrite.write("info@timeofsoftware.com\n")
fwrite.close()
print("### Updated file ###")
fread = open("test.txt","r")
text = fread.read()
fread.close()
print(text)
```

The execution of the above source code has the following output:

```
================= RESTART: /Users/alfre/Desktop/Python/8-2-1.py =================
### Initial file ###
Time of Software
http://www.timeofsoftware.com
Learn Python in a weekend
Python is cool

### Writting lines... ###

### Updated file ###
Time of Software
http://www.timeofsoftware.com
Learn Python in a weekend
Python is cool
info@timeofsoftware.com

>>>
```

125

The second exercise in the phase consists of learning to create files using the "**x**" opening mode. In the exercise, a file is going to create, and the information is going to write in it. Later we show the file content on the screen. The source code is as follows:

```
fcreation = open("creationtest.txt","x")
fcreation.write("Time of Software\n")
fcreation.write("File created 8-2-2\n")
fcreation.close()

print("### File created ###")

fread = open("creationtest.txt","r")
text = fread.read()
fread.close()
print(text)
```

The execution of the above source code has the following output:

```
================= RESTART: /Users/alfre/Desktop/Python/8-2-2.py =================
### File created ###
Time of Software
File created 8-2-2

>>>
```

As we mentioned in the theoretical part, the opening mode "**x**" returns an error if the file exists. The following image shows the error that would appear if you rerun the program.

```
================= RESTART: /Users/alfre/Desktop/Python/8-2-2.py =================
Traceback (most recent call last):
  File "/Users/alfre/Desktop/Python/8-2-2.py", line 1, in <module>
    fcreation = open("creationtest.txt","x")
FileExistsError: [Errno 17] File exists: 'creationtest.txt'
>>>
```

The third exercise of the phase consists of learning to write in text files by eliminating the content they previously had, that is, truncating it. This truncation does with the aperture mode "**w**". In the exercise, you write to an existing text file that truncates using the opening mode "**w**". Then the content is displayed on the screen.

126

The file used by the exercise is the one from the previous exercise. The source code is as follows:

```
fcreation = open("creationtest.txt","w")
fcreation.write("File created from scratch\n")
fcreation.write("Time of Software\n")
fcreation.write("File created 8-2-3\n")
fcreation.close()

print("### File created ###")

fread = open("creationtest.txt","r")
text = fread.read()
fread.close()
print(text)
```

The execution of the above source code has the following output:

```
================= RESTART: /Users/alfre/Desktop/Python/8-2-3.py =================
### File created ###
File created from scratch
Time of Software
File created 8-2-3

>>>
```

NOW YOU CAN...

In this eighth objective, you have learned the following knowledge:

- Creation of text files.
- Read from text files.
- Write in text files.

127

In this ninth objective, you are going to learn how to handle exceptions and errors that can occur in the programs you write.

The objective contains only one phase where you learn how to handle exceptions in Python.

## THEORETICAL CONCEPTS

In this section, we are going to explain the theoretical concepts that you have to know to work with exceptions.

## EXCEPTIONS

An exception is an error that occurs while the program is running, and that does not occur frequently.

The source code allows us to use operations called "**exception handling**". They are nothing more than saving the program state in the moment of the error and interrupting the program to execute some specific source code. In many cases, depending on the error that occurred, handling the exception means that the program continues to run after handling it. In many cases, this is not possible.

An example of an exception can be the division by 0.

The process of handling exceptions is similar in all programming languages. Firstly, it is necessary to include the execution source code within a block with the **try** statement. Then a code block is created within an **except** statement; it is the one executes in case of error. The **except** block allows you to specify the type of error that you control with the code block, which is why you can have as many **except** blocks as errors you want to control. However, it is also possible to control a generic error that includes all errors. In exception handling, it is possible to create a code block (**finally**) always executes at the end, regardless of whether an error occurs or not. This code block writes as part of the final statement.

Exception handling in Python looks like this:

*try:*
    *ProgramInstructionBlock*
*except ErrorType1:*
    *Error1InstructionBlock:*
*except ErrorType2:*
    *Error2InstructionBlock*
*except ErrorTypeN:*
    *ErrorNInstructionBlock*
*finally:*
    *FinallyInstructionBlock*

Let's look at each element in detail:

- try: start indicator of the source code block to be handled.
- ProgramInstructionBlock: the set of instructions that make up the program.
- except: it specifies the beginning of a handled exception.
- ErrorType: it specifies the type of error that handles *except*. The parameter is optional. If the type is not specified, the exception handles generically.
- ErrorInstructionBlock: the set of instructions that executes if the error indicated by ErrorType occurs.
- finally: the indicator for the beginning of the final code block. The section is optional.

- FinallyInstructionBlock: the set of instructions executed at the end of any of the previous code blocks.

In Python, there are different types of exceptions that can handle; all of them derive from a series of base exceptions. In the annexe at the end of the book, you can find the different types of exceptions that exist in Python.

## PHASE 1: HANDLING EXCEPTIONS

The first phase of the objective, and only one, consists of learning what an exception is, how it occurs and how to handle it.

The first exercise in the phase consists of executing a program composed only of an instruction that throws an exception, a division by zero. The source code is as follows:

```
print(3/0)
```

The execution of the above source code has the following output:

```
================ RESTART: /Users/alfre/Desktop/Python/9-1-1.py ================
Traceback (most recent call last):
  File "/Users/alfre/Desktop/Python/9-1-1.py", line 1, in <module>
    print(3/0)
ZeroDivisionError: division by zero
>>>
```

The second exercise in the phase consists of controlling the source code of the previous program and catching the exception that is thrown by division by zero. The objective is that the error from before does not display on the screen, and we show a custom message. The source code is as follows:

```
try:
    print(3/0)
except:
    print("ERROR: Division by zero")
```

The execution of the above source code has the following output:

```
================ RESTART: /Users/alfre/Desktop/Python/9-1-2.py ================
ERROR: Division by zero
>>>
```

The third exercise in the phase consists of including a final code block and indicating that the program has finished. The source code is as follows:

```
print("Program starting!")
try:
    print(3/0)
except:
    print("ERROR: Division by zero")
finally:
    print("Program finished!")
```

The execution of the above source code has the following output:

```
================ RESTART: /Users/alfre/Desktop/Python/9-1-3.py ================
Program starting!
ERROR: Division by zero
Program finished!
>>>
```

The fourth exercise of the phase consists of verifying that the code block that we have included in the final block also executes if the program does not throw an exception. For this, instead of dividing by zero, we are going to divide by one. The source code is as follows:

```
print("Program starting!")
try:
    print(3/1)
except:
    print("ERROR: Division by zero")
finally:
    print("Program finished!")
```

The execution of the above source code has the following output:

```
================ RESTART: /Users/alfre/Desktop/Python/9-1-4.py ================
Program starting!
3.0
Program finished!
>>>
```

The fifth exercise of the phase consists of adding an *else* instruction
block that executes when no exceptions are thrown. It means that
the instruction block contained in the *else* block executed when no
exceptions raised during the code execution. The source code is as
follows:

```
print("Program starting!")
try:
    print(3/1)
except:
    print("ERROR: Division by zero")
else:
    print("No errors!")
finally:
    print("Program finished!")
```

The execution of the above source code has the following output:

```
================ RESTART: /Users/alfre/Desktop/Python/9-1-5.py ================
Program starting!
3.0
No errors!
Program finished!
>>>
```

The sixth exercise of the phase consists of verifying that the block
of instructions that we have previously introduced inside *else* does
not execute if an exception occurs. To do this, we divide by zero
again instead of by one. The source code is as follows:

```
print("Program starting!")
try:
    print(3/0)
except:
    print("ERROR: Division by zero")
else:
    print("No errors!")
finally:
    print("Program finished!")
```

The execution of the above source code has the following output:

```
================ RESTART: /Users/alfre/Desktop/Python/9-1-6.py ================
Program starting!
ERROR: Division by zero
Program finished!
>>>
```

The seventh exercise of the phase is to learn how to specify the exception type that you want to handle. We are going to add a control for the exception type *ZeroDivisionError*. We keep the generic exception capture in case of another exception than the specific one could occur. In this way, we would specifically capture the exception of the division and generically the rest of the exceptions. The source code is as follows:

```
print("Program starting!")
try:
    print(3/0)
except ZeroDivisionError:
    print("ERROR: Division by zero")
except:
    print("ERROR: General error")
else:
    print("No errors!")
finally:
    print("Program finished!")
```

The execution of the above source code has the following output:

```
================ RESTART: /Users/alfre/Desktop/Python/9-1-7.py ================
Program starting!
ERROR: Division by zero
Program finished!
>>>
```

NOW YOU CAN...

In this ninth objective, you have learned the following knowledge:

- Source code control through exceptions.

Now it is the time to do the fourth project of the book, in which you are going to consolidate the knowledge acquired in handling exceptions from the previous objective.

The project consists of evolving project number two, including exception handling and reorganizing the source code adding a unique function to read the numbers, also with exception handling.

The objective of the project, in addition to practice the use of exception handling, is to familiarize you with a widely used concept in software development, which is the refactoring of source code. The code refactoring consists of modifying the source code without altering its behaviour. We use it to clean the source code, make the code more readable, improve its performance and its maintenance.

## SOURCE CODE AND EXECUTION

You are going to modify the source code of project number two by making the following changes:

- Include exception handling in the division function to control that if the user enters a zero as a divisor, the program does not return an error.
- Creation of a new function that performs the reading of numbers entered by users. The function has the following characteristics:
    - It receives as an input parameter the text to display to ask the user to enter the number.
    - It handles the exceptions of the introduction by the user values that are not number. The function ends once the user has entered a number, that is, it

continues to ask the user for the number until it enters it correctly.

o It returns the result of reading the number.

- Modify all the functions to read the numbers using the new function created for this purpose.

The resulting source code is as follows:

```
def ReadNumber(text):
    read = False
    while not read:
        try:
            number = int(input(text))
        except ValueError:
            print("Error: You have to enter a number.")
        else:
            read = True
    return number

def Sum():
    sum1 = ReadNumber("Sumand one (integer):")
    sum2 = ReadNumber("Sumand two (integer):")
    print ("Sum result:", sum1+sum2)

def Subtraction():
    minuend = ReadNumber("Minuend (integer):")
    subtrahend = ReadNumber("Subtrahend (integer):")
    print ("Subtraction result:", minuend-subtrahend)

def Multiplication():
    multiplying = ReadNumber("Multiplying (integer):")
    multiplier = ReadNumber("Multiplier (integer):")
    print ("Multiplication result:", multiplying*multiplier)

def Division():
    dividend = ReadNumber("Dividend (integer):")
    divider = ReadNumber("Divider (integer):")
    try:
        result = dividend/divider
    except ZeroDivisionError:
        print("Error: Division by zero not allowed.")
    else:
        print ("Division result:", result)
```

```python
def ShowMenu():
    print ("""************
Calculator
************
Menu
1) Sum
2) Subtraction
3) Multiplication
4) Division
5) Show menu
6) Exit""")

def Calculator():
    end = False
    ShowMenu()
    while not(end):
        opt = ReadNumber("Opcion:")
        if (opt==1):
            Sum()
        elif(opt==2):
            Subtraction()
        elif(opt==3):
            Multiplication()
        elif(opt==4):
            Division()
        elif(opt==5):
            ShowMenu()
        elif(opt==6):
            end = 1

Calculator()
```

The execution of the above source code has the following output:

```
=============== RESTART: /Users/alfre/Desktop/Python/Project4.py ===============
***********
Calculator
***********
Menu
1) Sum
2) Subtraction
3) Multiplication
4) Division
5) Show menu
6) Exit
Opcion:1
Sumand one (integer):R2D2
Error: You have to enter a number.
Sumand one (integer):67
Sumand two (integer):Hello
Error: You have to enter a number.
Sumand two (integer):89
Sum result: 156
Opcion:4
Dividend (integer):C3P0
Error: You have to enter a number.
Dividend (integer):33
Divider (integer):0
Error: Division by zero not allowed.
Opcion:6
>>>
```

## NOW YOU CAN...

In this fourth project, you have learned the following knowledge:

- Handle exceptions in programs that you already had developed.
- Source code refactor.

Now is the time to complete the final book project, in which you are going to use all the knowledge you have learned during the book.

## SOURCE CODE AND EXECUTION

In this section, we are going to explain the source code of the project with each of its components, and we run it so you can see how it works.

The Contacts project is composed of the following classes:

- **Address**: it contains all the information regarding an address.
- **Person**: it contains all the information regarding a person.
- **Telephone**: it contains all the information regarding the telephones.
- **Contact**: inherits from the three previous classes to form a class that contains all the information about a contact together.
- **ContactList**: it contains all the information of all the contacts.

Let's see the classes in detail:

### Address Class

The address class is composed of the following attributes:

- **Street**: it contains information regarding the street of the address.

- **Floor**: it contains information regarding the floor of the address.
- **City**: it contains information regarding the city of the address.
- **Postal Code**: it contains information regarding the postal code of the address.

The address class is composed of the following methods:

- **GetStreet**: it returns the information of the Street attribute.
- **GetFloor**: it returns the information of the Floor attribute.
- **GetCity**: it returns the information of the City attribute.
- **GetPostalCode**: it returns the information of the PostalCode attribute.
- **SetStreet**: it modifies the information of the Street attribute.
- **SetFloor**: it modifies the information of the Floor attribute.
- **SetCity**: it modifies the information of the City attribute.
- **SetPostalCode**: it modifies the information of the PostalCode attribute.

**Person class**

The person class is composed of the following attributes:

- **Name**: it contains information regarding the name of the person.
- **LastName**: it contains information regarding the last name of the person.
- **DateOfBirth**: it contains information regarding the person's date of birth.

The person class is composed of the following methods:

- **GetName**: it returns the information of the Name attribute.
- **GetLastName**: it returns the information of the LastName attribute.
- **GetDateOfBirth**: it returns the information of the DateOfBirth attribute.
- **SetName**: it modifies the information of the Name attribute.
- **SetLastName**: it modifies the information of the LastName attribute.
- **SetDateOfBirth**: it modifies the information of the DateOfBirth attribute.

**Phone class**

The phone class is composed of the following attributes:

- **House**: it contains information regarding the house phone.
- **Mobile**: it contains information regarding the mobile phone.
- **Work**: it contains information regarding the work phone.

The phone class is composed of the following methods:

- **GetHousePhone**: it returns the information of the House phone attribute.
- **GetMobilePhone**: it returns the information of the Mobile phone attribute.
- **GetWorkPhone**: it returns the information of the Work phone attribute.
- **SetHousePhone**: it modifies the information of the House phone attribute.
- **SetMobilePhone**: it modifies the information of the Mobile phone attribute.

- **SetWorkPhone**: it modifies the information of the Work phone attribute.

## Contact class

The contact class is composed of the following attributes:

- **Email**: contain information regarding the email.

The contact class is composed of the following methods:

- **GetEmail**: it returns the information from the Email attribute.
- **SetEmail**: it modifies the information of the Email attribute.
- **ShowContact**: it displays the complete information of the contact.

The contact class inherits from the previous ones. It means that added to its attributes and methods, it has the ones of inherited classes.

## ContactList class

The *ContactList* class is composed of the following attributes:

- **Contacts**: it contains information about all the contacts that are in the contact list.
- **Path**: it contains information about the physical path of the file on the computer where the contacts are stored.

The *ContactsList* class is composed of the following methods:

- **LoadContacts**: it loads the contact list into the application, reading it from the file.

- **CreateNewContact**: it stores a new contact in the Contacts attribute.
- **SaveContacts**: it saves in the file the list of contacts that the Contacts attribute stores.
- **ShowContactList**: it displays the content of the Contacts attribute on the screen.
- **SearchContactByName**: it searches for a contact in the Contacts attribute by name and returns it.
- **SearchContactByPhone**: it searches for a contact in the Contacts attribute by their phone and returns it.
- **DeleteContactByName**: it deletes a contact from the Contacts attribute using the name to search for it.
- **DeleteContactByPhone**: it deletes a contact from the Contacts attribute using the phone to search for it.

The class constructor receives as a parameter, the path where the file used to store the contacts located.

## Functions

Now let's see the different functions that the project contains:

- **ObtainOption**: it reads the option chosen from the menu by the user.
- **ShowMenu**: it displays the options menu on the screen.
- **SearchContacts**: it carries out the complete search process except for the search process in the list, which is carried out by the *ContactList* class with one of the search methods.
- **CreateNewContactProcess**: it carries out the complete process of creating a contact except for the storage in the list, done by the *ContactList* class.
- **DeleteContact**: it carries out the complete deleting process of contacts except for the deletion from the list, done by the *ContactList* class.

- **Main**: the main function of the application that contains the program flow.

The source code would be the following:

```
class Address:
    def __init__(self):
        self.__Street = ""
        self.__Floor = ""
        self.__City = ""
        self.__PostalCode = ""
    def GetStreet(self):
        return self.__Street
    def GetFloor(self):
        return self.__Floor
    def GetCity(self):
        return self.__City
    def GetPostalCode(self):
        return self.__PostalCode
    def SetStreet(self, street):
        self.__Street = street
    def SetFloor(self, floor):
        self.__Floor = floor
    def SetCity(self, city):
        self.__City = city
    def SetPostalCode(self, postalcode):
        self.__PostalCode = postalcode

class Person:
    def __init__(self):
        self.__Name = ""
        self.__LastName = ""
        self.__DateOfBirth = ""
    def GetName(self):
        return self.__Name
    def GetLastName(self):
        return self.__LastName
    def GetDateOfBirth(self):
        return self.__DateOfBirth
    def SetName(self, name):
        self.__Name = name
    def SetLastName(self, lastname):
        self.__LastName = lastname
    def SetDateOfBirth(self, dateofbirth):
        self.__DateOfBirth = dateofbirth
```

```python
class Phone:
    def __init__(self):
        self.__Mobile = ""
        self.__House = ""
        self.__Work = ""
    def GetMobilePhone(self):
        return self.__Mobile
    def GetHousePhone(self):
        return self.__House
    def GetWorkPhone(self):
        return self.__Work
    def SetMobilePhone(self, mobile):
        self.__Mobile = mobile
    def SetHousePhone(self, house):
        self.__House = house
    def SetWorkPhone(self, work):
        self.__Work = work

class Contact(Person, Address, Phone):
    def __init__(self):
        self.__Email = ""
    def GetEmail(self):
        return self.__Email
    def SetEmail(self, email):
        self.__Email = email
    def ShowContact(self):
        print("----- Contact -----")
        print("Name: ", self.GetName())
        print("Last name: ", self.GetLastName())
        print("Date of birth: ", self.GetDateOfBirth())
        print("Mobile phone: ", self.GetMobilePhone())
        print("House phone: ", self.GetHousePhone())
        print("Work phone: ", self.GetWorkPhone())
        print("Street: ", self.GetStreet())
        print("Floor: ", self.GetFloor())
        print("City: ", self.GetCity())
        print("Postal code: ", self.GetPostalCode())
        print("Email: ", self.__Email)
        print("-------------------")

class ContactList:
    def __init__(self, path):
        self.__Contacts = []
        self.__Path = path
    def LoadContacts(self):
        try:
```

144

```python
        f = open(self.__Path,"r")
    except:
        print("ERROR: File does not exist")
    else:
        contacts = f.readlines()
        f.close()
        if(len(contacts)>0):
            for contact in contacts:
                data = contact.split("#")
                if(len(data)==11):
                    newcontact = Contact()
                    newcontact.SetName(data[0])
                    newcontact.SetLastName(data[1])
                    newcontact.SetDateOfBirth(data[2])
                    newcontact.SetMobilePhone(data[3])
                    newcontact.SetHousePhone(data[4])
                    newcontact.SetWorkPhone(data[5])
                    newcontact.SetStreet(data[6])
                    newcontact.SetFloor(data[7])
                    newcontact.SetCity(data[8])
                    newcontact.SetPostalCode(data[9])
                    newcontact.SetEmail(data[10])
                    self.__Contacts = self.__Contacts + [newcontact]
            print("INFO: It has been loaded ",len(self.__Contacts)," contacts.")
def CreateNewContact(self,newcontact):
    self.__Contacts = self.__Contacts + [newcontact]
def SaveContacts(self):
    try:
        f = open(self.__Path,"w")
    except:
        print("ERROR: The information can not be saved.")
    else:
        for contact in self.__Contacts:
            text = contact.GetName() + "#"
            text = text + contact.GetLastName() + "#"
            text = text + contact.GetDateOfBirth() + "#"
            text = text + contact.GetMobilePhone() + "#"
            text = text + contact.GetHousePhone() + "#"
            text = text + contact.GetWorkPhone() + "#"
            text = text + contact.GetStreet() + "#"
            text = text + contact.GetFloor() + "#"
            text = text + contact.GetCity() + "#"
            text = text + contact.GetPostalCode() + "#"
            text = text + contact.GetEmail() + "\n"
            f.write(text)
        f.close()
def ShowContactList(self):
```

145

```python
        print("########## CONTACT LIST ##########")
        print("Number of contacts: ",len(self.__Contacts))
        for contact in self.__Contacts:
            contact.ShowContact()
        print("#########################")
    def SearchContactByName(self, name):
        foundlist = []
        for contact in self.__Contacts:
            if contact.GetName() == name:
                foundlist = foundlist + [contact]
        return foundlist
    def SearchContactByPhone(self, phone):
        foundlist = []
        for contact in self.__Contacts:
            if (contact.GetMobilePhone() == phone
                or contact.GetHousePhone() == phone
                or contact.GetWorkPhone() == phone):
                foundlist = foundlist + [contact]
        return foundlist
    def DeleteContactByName(self, name):
        finallist = []
        for contact in self.__Contacts:
            if contact.GetName() != name:
                finallist = finallist + [contact]
        print("INFO: ", len(self.__Contacts) - len(finallist)," contacts deleted")
        self.__Contacts = finallist
    def DeleteContactByPhone(self, phone):
        finallist = []
        for contact in self.__Contacts:
            if (contact.GetMobilePhone() != phone
                and contact.GetHousePhone() != phone
                and contact.GetWorkPhone() != phone):
                finallist = finallist + [contact]
        print("INFO: ", len(self.__Contacts) - len(finallist)," contacts deleted")
        self.__Contacts = finallist

def ObtainOption(text):
    read = False
    while not read:
        try:
            number = int(input(text))
        except ValueError:
            print("ERROR: You have to enter a number.")
        else:
            read = True
    return number
```

```
def ShowMenu():
    print ("""Menu
1) Show list of contacts
2) Search contacts
3) Create a new contact
4) Delete contacts
5) Save contacts
6) Exit""")

def SearchContacts(contacts):
    print ("""Search contacts by:
1) Name
2) Phone
3) Back""")
    endsearch = False
    while not endsearch:
        option = ObtainOption("Option:")
        if option == 1:
            founds = contacts.SearchContactByName(input((">Enter the name to search: ")))
            if len(founds) > 0:
                print("########## CONTACTS FOUND ##########")
                for item in founds:
                    item.ShowContact()
                    print("########################################")
            else:
                print("INFO: No contacts found")
            endsearch = True
        elif option == 2:
            founds = contacts.SearchContactByPhone(input((">Enter the phone to search: ")))
            if len(founds) > 0:
                print("########## CONTACTS FOUND ##########")
                for item in founds:
                    item.ShowContact()
                    print("########################################")
            else:
                print("INFO: No contacts found")
            endsearch = True
        elif option == 3:
            endsearch = True

def CreateNewContactProcess(contacts):
    newcontact = Contact()
    newcontact.SetName(input((">Enter the name: ")))
    newcontact.SetLastName(input((">Enter the last name: ")))
    newcontact.SetDateOfBirth(input((">Enter the date of birth: ")))
    newcontact.SetMobilePhone(input((">Enter the mobile phone: ")))
    newcontact.SetHousePhone(input((">Enter the house phone: ")))
```

```python
        newcontact.SetWorkPhone(input((">Enter the work phone: ")))
        newcontact.SetStreet(input((">Enter the address: ")))
        newcontact.SetFloor(input((">Enter the floor: ")))
        newcontact.SetCity(input((">Enter the city: ")))
        newcontact.SetPostalCode(input((">Enter the postal code: ")))
        newcontact.SetEmail(input((">Enter the email: ")))
        contacts.CreateNewContact(newcontact)

def DeleteContact(contacts):
    print ("""Search contacts by:
1) Name
2) Phone
3) Back""")
    end = False
    while not end:
        option = ObtainOption("Option:")
        if option == 1:
            contacts.DeleteContactByName(input((">Enter the name to use to delete: ")))
            end = True
        elif option == 2:
            contacts.DeleteContactByPhone(input((">Enter the phone to use to delete: ")))
            end = True
        elif option == 3:
            end = True

def Main():
    contacts = ContactList("contacts.txt")
    contacts.LoadContacts()
    end = False
    while not(end):
        ShowMenu()
        option = ObtainOption("Option:")
        if (option==1):
            contacts.ShowContactList()
        elif(option==2):
            SearchContacts(contacts)
        elif(option==3):
            CreateNewContactProcess(contacts)
        elif(option==4):
            DeleteContact(contacts)
        elif(option==5):
            contacts.SaveContacts()
        elif(option==6):
            end = 1

Main()
```

Before executing the source code, you must create the empty "contacts.txt" file and modify the first line of the Main function in which the path of the file to the ContactList class indicated by parameter.

Next, we show you an example of creating a contact and showing the contacts in the contact list, options 3 and 1 of the menu.

```
============= RESTART: /Users/alfre/Desktop/Python/FinalProject.py =============
INFO: It has been loaded  0  contacts.
Menu
1) Show list of contacts
2) Search contacts
3) Create a new contact
4) Delete contacts
5) Save contacts
6) Exit
Option:3
>Enter the name: Alfredo
>Enter the last name: Moreno
>Enter the date of birth: 10/05/1984
>Enter the mobile phone: 987654321
>Enter the house phone: 123456789
>Enter the work phone: 546372819
>Enter the address: Fake Street 123
>Enter the floor: 4
>Enter the city: Madrid
>Enter the postal code: 28850
>Enter the email: info@timeofsoftware.com
Menu
1) Show list of contacts
2) Search contacts
3) Create a new contact
4) Delete contacts
5) Save contacts
6) Exit
Option:1
########## CONTACT LIST ##########
Number of contacts:  1
----- Contact -----
Name:  Alfredo
Last name:  Moreno
Date of birth:  10/05/1984
Mobile phone:  987654321
House phone:  123456789
Work phone:  546372819
Street:  Fake Street 123
Floor:  4
City:  Madrid
Postal code:  28850
Email:  info@timeofsoftware.com
--------------------
#############################
```

The following screenshot shows the option to search for a contact by name, option 2 of the menu.

```
============== RESTART: /Users/alfre/Desktop/Python/FinalProject.py =============
INFO: It has been loaded  1   contacts.
Menu
1) Show list of contacts
2) Search contacts
3) Create a new contact
4) Delete contacts
5) Save contacts
6) Exit
Option:4
Search contacts by:
1) Name
2) Phone
3) Back
Option:2
>Enter the phone to use to delete: 987654321
INFO:  1   contacts deleted
Menu
1) Show list of contacts
2) Search contacts
3) Create a new contact
4) Delete contacts
5) Save contacts
6) Exit
Option:1
########## CONTACT LIST ##########
Number of contacts:  0
############################
```

The following screenshot shows the option to delete a contact by name, option 4 from the menu.

## NOW YOU CAN...

In this final project, you have learned the following knowledge:

- Carry out a complete program with all the knowledge acquired in the book.

Congratulations! You have reached the end of the learning! So that you are aware of everything you have learned in a weekend, we have prepared a summary of the milestones you have reached:

- Display information on the screen in one line and multiple lines.
- Read the information entered by users through the keyboard.
- Use of variables.
- Existing data types in Python.
- Data conversion.
- Use of integer and real numbers.
- Use of mathematical, relational and logical operators.
- Use of booleans.
- Use of text strings and their manipulation.
- Use of lists, tuples and dictionaries.
- Use of all variants of the *if* bifurcations.
- Use of *for* and *while* loops.
- Creation and use of functions.
- Use of classes in your programs.
- Difference between class and object or instance.
- Creation of classes.
- Access to public and private class attributes and methods.
- Use of class composition.
- Use of multiple and simple inheritances of classes.
- Creation of files.
- Reading and write information from/in files.
- Source code control through exceptions.
- Carry out a complete program with all the knowledge acquired in the book.

In the Annexes section, we explain theoretical concepts that expand the knowledge acquired throughout the book.

## RESERVED WORDS

Some of the reserved words explained here have not been covered in the book as they are outside its scope. The objective of the annexe is to offer you the list of reserved words in case you need to consult it in the future.

The list of Python reserved words that cannot use as names of variables, functions, classes, attributes, and methods are as follows:

- **and**: logical representation of AND.
- **as**: it has two functions, the first one is to assign an exception to a specific object and the second one is to rename a module imported into the code.
- **assert**: used in code debugging to throw errors if certain conditions are right.
- **break**: used to end a loop.
- **class**: used to define a class.
- **continue**: it suspends the iteration of a loop and jumps to the next iteration of it.
- **def**: used to define functions.
- **del**: it has two functions, the first one is to remove the reference of a specific object and the second one is to remove items from a list.
- **elif**: definition of an alternative bifurcation with a condition.
- **else**: definition of the path without condition at a bifurcation.

- **except**: used to catch exceptions that occurred during the execution of the source code.
- **False**: used to represent the Boolean value 0 / false.
- **finally**: used to define a block of source code that executes at the end of exception processing.
- **for**: used to define for loops.
- **from**: used to import elements of external modules into our code.
- **global**: used to modify objects in a lower scope, creating a new object and without altering the value of the object in the upper scope.
- **if**: it defines a bifurcation with a condition.
- **import**: import an external module to our code. It can be used together with *from*, but in that case, it imports elements instead of the entire module.
- **in**: determines the existence of an element in a list, tuple, dictionary or any iterable object.
- **is**: determines if two objects are equal. Two objects with the same values are not the same as two equal objects.
- **lambda**: used to define lambda functions.
- **None**: represents the absence of value.
- **nonlocal**: allows you to modify the value of an object defined in a previous scope.
- **not**: logical representation of NOT.
- **or**: logical representation of OR.
- **pass**: it only has aesthetic functions to fill gaps in the source code.
- **print**: used to print a text string on the screen.
- **raise**: used to raise exceptions.
- **return**: used to return an element at the end of the execution of a function/method.
- **True**: used to represent the Boolean value 1 / true.

- **try**: used to define instruction blocks with exception handling.
- **while**: used to define while loops.
- **with**: used to encapsulate the execution of a source code block.
- **yield**: used to return more than one element at the end of the execution of a function.

## CODE COMMENTS

A resource used in programming to clarify the source code that you write is the use of comments. Comments are a way of adding documentation to the source code files. For example: explaining what a function does, explaining the input parameters it has and the output parameters that it returns when it finishes the execution.

The comments, when executing the program, are ignored by the computer, so you can enter all the comments you want or need. However, we recommend you to write descriptive code, both at the level of names that you choose for variables, functions or classes as at the level of the instructions themselves.

Comments can add to the source code in two different ways:

- **Single-line comments**: these usually refer to a single statement in the source code. In Python, you have to write the character '#' at the beginning of the line to indicate that this line is a comment.
- **Comment block or multi-line comment**: these usually refer to a block of instructions, although they can also be used only to one line. In Python, you have to put the characters """ (triple-double quote) at the beginning of the first line of the block and the end of the last line of the block.

The following example shows a single line comment:

```
sumand1 = float(input("First summand: "))
sumand2 = float(input("Second summand: "))
# Once we have both values we add them
print("Result: ", sumand1 + sumand2)
```

The following example shows a comment block:

```
""" The next source code performs the addition of
the two numbers requested to the user"""
sumand1 = float(input("First summand: "))
sumand2 = float(input("Second summand: "))
print("Result: ", sumand1 + sumand2)
```

## SPECIAL CHARACTERS IN STRINGS

In this annexe, we are going to explain a set of special/escape characters that you can use in text strings.

The characters are as follows:

- \\: character to insert the slash \ in the text string.
- \': character to insert a single quote in the text string.
- \": character to insert a double quote in the text string.
- \a: character to insert the ASCII character Bell in the text string.
- \b: character to insert the ASCII Backspace character in the text string.
- \f: character to insert a page break in the text string.
- \n: character to insert a line break in the text string.
- \r: character to insert a carriage break in the text string.
- \t: character to insert a horizontal tab stop in the text string.
- \uxxxx: character to enter a 16-bit hexadecimal character. It is only valid for Unicode character sets.

155

- **\Uxxxxxxxx**: character to enter a 32-bit hexadecimal character. It is only valid for Unicode character sets.
- **\v**: character to insert a vertical tab in the text string.
- **\ooo**: character to insert an octal character in the text string.
- **\xhh**: character to insert a hexadecimal character in the text string.

Escape characters enter in the same way as other characters in text strings.

## EXISTING EXCEPTIONS IN PYTHON

In this annexe, we are going to explain the different exceptions that you can use in Python. The list includes all the existing ones, so it includes exceptions related to concepts that are outside the scope of the book.

We show two different lists of exceptions, the first one includes generic exceptions, and the second one includes specific exceptions derived from the generic ones.

**Generic exceptions:**

- **Exception**: more generic type of exception, from which all existing exceptions in Python derive.
- **ArithmeticError**: generic exception type for arithmetic errors.
- **BufferError**: generic exception type for errors related to buffers.
- **LookupError**: generic exception type for errors related to access to collection data.

**Specific exceptions:**

- **AssertionError**: thrown when the assert instruction fails.
- **AttributeError**: thrown when there is an error when assigning a value to an attribute or when trying to access it.
- **EOFError**: thrown when reading from a file does not return data.
- **FloatingPointError**: exception not used.
- **GeneratorExit**: thrown when a function of type generator or coroutine is closed.
- **ImportError**: thrown when trying to import a module into the program and it fails.
- **ModuleNotFoundError**: thrown when trying to import a module and it cannot find. It derives from the previous one.
- **IndexError**: thrown when trying to access a position in a collection and the index is higher than the most significant position.
- **KeyError**: thrown when trying to access a dictionary key and it does not exist.
- **KeyboardInterrupt**: thrown when the user uses the interrupt command with the keyboard (Control-C or delete).
- **MemoryError**: thrown when the program executes an instruction and it exceeds the maximum available memory.
- **NameError**: thrown when the local or global name does not exist.
- **NotImplementedError**: thrown when a method of a class is not implemented yet.
- **OSError**: thrown when the operating system throws an exception when executing an instruction. These are the specific exceptions that the operating system can throw:
  - ○ **BlockingIOError**: thrown when an operation blocked on an object that should not be blocked.
  - ○ **ChildProcessError**: thrown when an operation of a child process returns an error.

- o **ConnectionError**: generic exception thrown for connection-related errors.
- o **BrokenPipeError**: thrown when trying to write to a socket and it has already been closed.
- o **ConnectionAbortedError**: thrown when during a connection attempt it is aborted by the other side of the connection.
- o **ConnectionRefusedError**: thrown when during a connection attempt is rejected by the other side of the connection.
- o **ConnectionResetError**: thrown when the connection resets by the other side of the connection.
- o **FileExistsError**: thrown when trying to create a file or directory and it already exists.
- o **FileNotFoundError**: thrown when trying to access a file or directory and it does not exist.
- o **IsADirectoryError**: thrown when trying to execute an operation related to files on a directory.
- o **NotADirectoryError**: thrown when trying to execute a directory-related operation on something that is not a directory.
- o **PermissionError**: thrown when trying to execute an operation and not having sufficient permissions.
- o **ProcessLookupError**: thrown when a process that does not exist is executed and has indicated that it does.
- o **TimeoutError**: thrown when the waiting time exceeded in some system function.
- **OverflowError**: thrown when the result of a mathematical operation is too large to be represented.
- **RecursionError**: thrown when the number of recursions exceeds the maximum allowed.

- **ReferenceError**: thrown when trying to access specific attributes by the proxy class and that are already in the garbage collector.
- **RuntimeError**: thrown when the error that occurs cannot categorize into any of the existing types.
- **StopIteration**: thrown when trying to access the next element of an iterator, and it does not have more elements to iterate over.
- **StopAsyncIteration**: thrown when trying to access the next element of an asynchronous iterator and it does not have more elements to iterate over.
- **SyntaxError**: thrown when the parser encounters a syntax error.
- **IndentationError**: thrown when the source code has indentation errors.
- **TabError**: thrown when the source code has tabulation errors.
- **SystemError**: thrown when the Python interpreter encounters an internal error while executing the program.
- **SystemExit**: thrown when executing the *sys.exit()* instruction and that causes the execution of the program to stop.
- **TypeError**: thrown when an operation or function uses an incorrect data type.
- **UnboundLocalError**: thrown when a local variable used in a function or method and no value previously assigned.
- **UnicodeError**: thrown when an error occurs when encoding or decoding Unicode.
- **UnicodeEncodeError**: thrown when an error occurs when encoding to Unicode.
- **UnicodeDecodeError**: thrown when an error occurs when decoding from Unicode.

- **UnicodeTranslateError**: thrown when an error occurs when translating to Unicode.

- **ValueError**: thrown when an operation or function receives a parameter of the correct type, but with an incorrect value.

- **ZeroDivisionError**: thrown when dividing by zero.

# ABOUT THE AUTHORS AND ACKNOWLEDGMENTS

This book and all about Time of Software is the result of many years dedicated to technological teaching. First with groups in secondary schools and later by teaching trainers.

The work of creating the learning method, synthesizing and organizing all the technical information related to Python and elaborating the different practices presented in the book is the responsibility of the people directly responsible of **Time of Software**, Alfredo Moreno and Sheila Córcoles. We are passionate about the technological world and teaching.

We want to thank our families, friends and co-workers for the unconditional support and contributions they have made to the Python learning method that we have developed. Thank you for being our guinea pigs! Without you, this would not have been possible.

And of course, thanks to you for purchasing "Learn Python in a weekend". We hope you had achieved the goal you set for yourself when you bought the book. You may have seen that this is only the beginning, that Python is an exciting world. Do not hesitate to contact us and how you are doing. **YOU ARE NOT ALONE!**

## DOWNLOADABLE MATERIAL

The source code of all the exercises carried out in the book can be downloaded from the following URL:

http://timeofsoftware.com/learn-python-exercises/

Printed in Great Britain
by Amazon